REPORT ON MYSELF WITHDRAWN

BOOKS BY GRÉGOIRE BOUILLIER

The Mystery Guest
Report on Myself

REPORT ON MYSELF

GRÉGOIRE BOUILLIER

Translated from the French by
BRUCE BENDERSON

MARINER BOOKS
Houghton Mifflin Harcourt
Boston   New York   2009

First Mariner Books edition 2009

Copyright © 2002 by Éditions Allia
Translation copyright © 2008 by Bruce Benderson
Originally published in 2002 by Éditions Allia, France, as *Rapport sur moi*

For information about permission to reproduce selections from this book,
write to Permissions, Houghton Mifflin Harcourt Publishing Company,
215 Park Avenue South, New York, New York 10003.

www.hmhbooks.com

Library of Congress Cataloging-in-Publication Data

Bouillier, Grégoire.
  [Rapport sur moi. English]
  Report on myself / Grégoire Bouillier.
      p. cm.
  ISBN-13: 978-0-618-96861-9
  ISBN-10: 0-618-96861-X
  1. Bouillier, Grégoire. 2. Authors, French—20th century—Biography
3. Authors, French—21st century—Biography I. Title.
  PQ2702.082Z46 2009
  843'.92 a B—dc22

Book design by Anne Chalmers
Text type: Bodoni Book

Printed in the United States of America
MP 10 9 8 7 6 5 4 3 2 1

Frederick II happened to get hold of a copy of one of Diderot's works. His eyes fell on the words: "To young people . . ." whereupon he closed the book, quite aware that it wasn't addressed to him.

—Prince de Ligne

REPORT ON MYSELF

I HAD A HAPPY childhood.

Sunday afternoon, my mother bolts into our room while
my brother and I are playing in our separate corners.
"Children, do I love you?" Her voice is intense, her nos-
trils beyond belief. My brother answers straight on, but all
I can muster with the confidence of my seven years is to
hem and haw. I get what's going on but at the same time
dread what's to follow. I end up murmuring, "Maybe you
love us a little too much." My mother looks at me in horror.
For a moment she's at a loss, then moves to the window,
shoves it open, and tries to throw herself from the sixth
floor. Having heard the noise, my father catches her on the
balcony after she has already stuck a leg into space. My
mother yells, puts up a fight. Her screams echo through
the courtyard. My father pulls her roughly backward and

1

drags her inside like a sack. During the struggle, my mother's head hits the wall and goes *clunk*. For a long time afterward, there's a small bloodstain on the wall. One day I draw some circles around it with a black felt-tip pen and use it as a dart target; when I hit the bull's-eye, I imagine for a brief instant finding again a way to speak without fear.

When my mother met my father, she was sixteen and he was eighteen. It was in 1956, during a surprise party at the house in Bois-Colombes into which my father's family had moved after the war in '39. My father brought the party to life by playing drums in a little jazz band made up of fellow law students. My mother helped him do the dishes; a year later they were married and they had my brother, whom they named Olivier for no particular reason I'm aware of.

My father barely had time to see his son; he had to do his compulsory military service. It wasn't the best moment to be drafted: instead of the obligatory eighteen months, what wasn't yet called the Algerian War forced him to wear a uniform for nearly three years. He was quartered at Tizi Ouzou, the capital of Algeria's Great Kabylia region, where, according to him, not much happened.

Getting separated from her husband so soon upset my mother. She quickly made up her mind: to abandon

2

her baby at her in-laws' and go join her lover in Algeria. Such boldness wasn't common to most seventeen-year-old girls of the time.

Down there, they loved each other. And they were more — *or should I say three times more?* — than happy to do so because an intern at the hospital in Tizi Ouzou fell under my mother's not unsubstantial charms; soon he'd join them in their romps, and in the midst of such threesomes, I was conceived.

"You're a love child," my mother would repeat to me throughout my childhood, without my knowing what it meant and whether it was something to worry about. In public she loved to mention my olive skin and the fact that there was no Bouillier in me. Much later, when I asked, she revealed the circumstances under which I was conceived and ended up saying that she'd read in a magazine that when two men ejaculate in a woman's vagina, instead of competing, their sperm cells fuse to fertilize the egg and give birth to a mutant.

She also told me that my father had great hard-ons and was a homosexual; later she claimed she'd said that to please me.

My mother was acting true to form; she wasn't yet twelve when her brother, who was two years older, stood up from the table and blurted at the father who was reprimanding him for some petty offense, "You're not my father!" In fact, he was their uncle; he'd secretly replaced their father in his sister-in-law's bed after their father had disappeared during the beginning of World War II. My mother, who was born at the end of 1939, hardly had a chance to know the man who'd given her life. She must have sensed it vaguely when she decided to go to Algeria to be with a man who himself had left for war right after the birth of his child. And just as a brother had stood in for another as her father, it was in the arms of two different men that she became a mother for the second time.

From brother to brother, my granny remained with the Pérards, and she didn't have to change names to keep appearing wonderfully married in the eyes of the world. All in all, it was kept in the family, and administratively it simplified things. Nevertheless, all traces of the one who disappeared had to be erased, which must have taken a certain effort, since it involved silencing a brother, a husband, and a father at the same time. The children were raised according to this little scheme.

For years on end, none of them suspected the truth except the elder, certain of whose confused memories couldn't be manipulated. In the case of my mother, she still remembers that discovering her life was built on a sham came as "a shock." In saying so, she can look me in the eye without getting flustered.

As for my granddad, he was an affable man, and he adored his little bastard bitch who followed him everywhere like a shadow. He dubbed her Satellite in honor, he claimed, of the Soviet satellite *Soyuz*, which means "union"; genitally speaking, this was pretty appropriate, and twenty times a day he could call the truth by its name, which he kept on a leash without anyone suspecting—not even him. When he shouted "Satellite," it came out "Slattern."

In Old French, Pérard means "bad father."

As for Bouillier, it means "small birch forest." Thus I know what kind of fiber I'm made of, which not everyone can say.

WHEN I WAS BORN, it was agreed that I'd be named Nicolas; but Brigitte Bardot had just had a child named Nicolas, so my mother immediately changed my first name to Grégoire. That's how I became "the one who stays awake, the wide-awake one," the etymology of Grégoire, which is from the Greek *egregorien.* If I'd been named Nicolas, I would have been endowed with the "victory of the people," which doesn't spell out the same destiny. To convince myself of it, I've sometimes become the friend of a Nicolas, who never figures out what our friendship owes to his first name. But I never met a Nicolas who considered the people dear to his heart, and even less their victory.

Contrary to tradition, my parents gave me no second name to follow Grégoire. So no ancestor, good or bad, ended up related to me. Nobody dead whose memory I'm supposed to honor. The honor of one day naming my shadow passed to me alone.

When I came out of my mother's belly, I was, supposedly, laughing. The midwives almost started arguing over who'd take care of me: they'd never seen a baby so happy about coming into the world.

Three days later, I weighed less than two pounds and was in an appalling state. It was because my mother, suffering from an abscess on her breast, couldn't nurse me, and I flatly turned down the commercial brand of milk, known as Guigoz. Neither cow's nor ass's milk worked any better. They were thinking I wouldn't last another day when I condescended to swallow the milk of a goat that they'd found almost by chance near the hospital. I owe my survival to that animal with a filthy reputation.

In Tizi Ouzou, it was 104 degrees in the shade the day I was born. "I never suffered as much as I did that day," my mother is happy to recount. She likes to remind me that I was so enormous near the end of her pregnancy that when she ate, she could balance her plate on her stomach.

Just as the case had been at the birth of her first child, my mother never doubted that she'd have a son. "I'm incapable of having a girl," she liked to say proudly. Which didn't prevent her from curling my hair with BaByliss when the whim seized her. She also says that she never wanted a third child, convinced as she was that it would be a deformed Mongoloid. One time I heard her guffaw, "I'm a regular rabbit," using that colorful expression to describe her gift for getting pregnant the minute she had sex, and even sometimes during her period. She's stopped remembering how many times she's had an abortion. At least fifteen times, she admits without embarrassment. Sometimes my father would help her. Together they experimented with various techniques. It happened in the afternoon when my brother and I were in school. Once, when my mother had to do it alone, she sloshed a few quarts of Mercurochrome into her vagina to make the fetus come out. She was saved from internal hemorrhaging only at the last minute.

My birth put an end to my parents' Algerian episode. Now responsible for a second child, my father was, as a result, discharged from military duty; for him, the war was over, without his having to fire a single shot. That was the first effect of my appearance on earth. My parents could even rejoice about producing a happy event

8

during a time that was being called "eventful" and certainly wasn't very happy. On the other hand, they had to give up that Franco-Algerian rapprochement they were having such a good time consecrating in bed. In fact, my mother refused to remain in Great Kabylia, even though her lover was begging her to, so the trio was torn apart, and its existence is kept alive only in my mother's eyes when she gazes at me.

For a long time my mother refused to tell me the name of that hospital intern in Tizi Ouzou. When she finally came out with it, I wrote it in a notebook and forgot about it. I never made an attempt to get to know him. Nor he me.

What's left for me from the circumstances of my birth is the feeling of being a child of a war, which, like so many other conflicts, never revealed its true purpose. Like a perception of history that clashes with the official version because it's less inane and morbid than that given by the people responsible for writing it. Similarly, when the times reached that supposed stage of "sexual liberation," I was already the result of it, and my parents hadn't needed any slogan for their unbridled pleasure. As far as I was concerned, Boccaccio and Aristophanes weren't far off the mark; nor were Sade and Georges Bataille, and especially the latter because he had the same initials as me.

In the family record book kept by my parents, it's written that I was born on June 22, 1960. In school I learned very early that Galileo had recanted on June 22, 1633, before the Roman Catholic Inquisition; and on June 22, 1940, Pétain signed the armistice with Hitler in a railroad car. To console myself, I've become used to writing my birth date algebraically; perfectly balanced, the order of the numerals 06 22 60 seems to contain a mysterious arithmetical palindrome, this time favorably distinguishing me from the lot.

In accordance with the Gregorian calendar, 1960 was a leap year; thus summer begins on June 22. I'm the one who makes the days get longer, I've been boasting for a long time. When life gets darker for me, I prefer to say that I'm shortening the nights.

The three women with whom I've lived up to this point have at least two points in common; they all maintain confrontational relationships with their fathers, and each of them was born between mid-September and mid-October; in other words, around nine months before the month of June. Moreover, between them and me, there's always been winter and spring to get through.

The one whose birth date is the closest to the time I was conceived was born on September 18. Just about four more days and I would have believed I was in the presence of the mystery of the incarnation of my soul, so to speak. She was born in 1968; so I was eight at the time, and nine months later I'd be nine. But, at that very moment Marie-Blanche disappeared forever, and for me she was the first among all of them. I've often thought that these two events were linked and that the soul who had just appeared on earth stood for the disappearance of the other in order to respect a certain balance, if not in the universe, then at least in my life.

I WAS THREE WEEKS OLD when a Bréguet twin-engined plane took my parents and me from Algiers to Lyon, where my godfather had agreed to pick us up. Our flight was hit by a storm that my parents remember to this day. I wailed throughout the trip. Every part of the plane groaned, tossed about by rain amid bursts of lightning. The captain deemed it necessary to come and reassure his passengers in person. He bent over my bassinet to calm me; I cried even harder.

That turbulent voyage must have left its marks: throughout my childhood I had the same nightmare about a grimacing face above my bed that suddenly rushed toward me at high speed, yet infinitely slowly. And after that, I never left one lover for another, nor changed my life or situation, without everything turning stormy. My idea of change is inseparable from a feeling of chaos. It's even to the point where turmoil can sometimes make me believe in change itself. If the skies between Algiers and Lyon had been fair, I sometimes think I would have come through certain events, and maybe even life itself, smoothly.

My godfather lived on the outskirts of Lyon in the castle of the chevalier de la Barre, famous for having been the last torture victim of the ancien régime after he'd considered it beneath him to remove his hat as a religious procession was passing by. A big park surrounded the castle, a kind of little manor from the eighteenth century that the town council of Vaulx-en-Velin tore down in 1974 in favor of an apple-green building whose ugliness has become common and which today still houses a community movie theater. The fields that extended around the castle in 1961 are now blocks and villages of public housing projects that for miles on end almost drive you nuts with boredom.

My parents lived in one wing of the castle, my godfather and his young wife in another. This carefree, romantic lifestyle would last a year. For his wife's birthday, my godfather bought her a little car, the kind she'd been dreaming of. The first time she took it out, she hit a plane tree and died instantly. My godfather never got over the fact that he'd given his wife death as a present and loathed everything around him. My parents had to leave. They never again saw the person who was supposed to vouch for my religious instruction.

My parents found a place to live in the Croix-Rousse section of Lyon, inside the city limits. It wasn't that easy. They had no money; my father had broken with his family after dressing down his father for marrying a "Negress." Nor could my mother count on her parents, whose worker salaries from the chain of Michelin factories barely met their own needs. So while my father looked for work, my mother went from one small hotel to another, looking for a room for the night; she had to go to a new one almost every day because my presence in such establishments wasn't exactly appreciated. Luckily, I was a very well behaved baby, and most of the time my mother managed to conceal my presence, hiding me inside a bag when she passed by the manager's desk.

My parents have very often told me the story of once being totally broke and not eating for three days so that they could keep what little money they had left for my bottles.

Totally drained of resources, my father finally contacted his. The latter promised to help him financially provided that he "change his nigger tune." My father put away his war drums, and we moved to Bois-Colombes, where I discovered that I had a brother two and a half years older than me, and he discovered that he had a younger brother and parents.

For his forty-fifth birthday, I gave my father a mini–drum set; he played it that evening, then the next day put it away in the attic for good.

During certain fun-filled and well-wined dinners, hearing a jazz number on the radio, my father would open a package of spaghetti, separate it into two fistfuls, and use it as drumsticks on the table, plates, and glasses; the more he'd swing, the more the spaghetti would break and go flying in every direction; by the end of the piece, there was nothing left in his hands. For days afterward, we'd keep finding bits of spaghetti on the carpet.

Our house in Bois-Colombes was too big to heat in winter. Mornings you had to clap your hands and stamp your feet on the staircase that led to the kitchen, to scare away the mice.

My brother and I had a babysitter. Her name was Madame Guillaumot. My brother admitted to me years later that his predilection for men may have stemmed from this last name, the pronunciation of which in French sounds like "Guy-homo": his first lover was called Guy.

I have no memory of Madame Guillaumot, except for a blurry one about her slapping me so hard that I fell off my baby chair and split my forehead. Madame Guillaumot explained to my parents that I'd banged it against the edge of the refrigerator all by myself. The lie left me with a scar that even today looks like it happened yesterday. As if my head refused to be sewn back together, with that base deed locked inside.

In all the photos of me as a child, that scar is concealed by bangs that hide my forehead; when I left my parents', I pushed my hair back, and it appeared for all to see, fresh and pink, never closed over.

Nevertheless, it isn't unusual for people who've known me for a long time to become surprised by that wound on my forehead. They never noticed it before and think it's recent. So I tell them that my mother bit me.

WE MOVED TO AUBERVILLIERS. One evening my mother came back from work and lay down to rest for a moment. My father had left to pick up my brother and me at the babysitter's. Suddenly she heard me call "Mommy" three times; my voice sounded so clear that in her drowsiness she thought we'd come back without her having noticed and that I was calling her from the edge of her bed. But it was dark, and the apartment was empty. At that exact moment the telephone rang and my father announced that I'd just been admitted to the hospital emergency room. My face disfigured by sores, I could no longer breathe, and I was close to suffocating. The doctors feared diphtheria, which at the time was lethal.

To prevent contagion, I was put in quarantine in a sterile room. My parents couldn't come near me and stood behind a window, sending me silent kisses that rarely reached me. Only gloved and masked nurses had the right to be there. My mother wept to see me in such a state. Her love, for once, was powerless.

This total isolation would last for seven days and seven nights, during which I continued to decline to such a degree in that coffin of glass that I came close to dying. I was barely four years old.

Tests finally revealed that I'd contracted staphylococcus aureus. Recently put on the market, penicillin rapidly got the better of my disease. However, I lost my sense of smell, which no one realized. And I hid it for a long time, using various strategies I'd developed. For example, I'd enthusiastically declare that the salad had a nice lemony taste after having come across a seed in the vinaigrette. If I've ever been intelligent, it's been by deceiving my world into thinking I've become so: into believing that I hadn't had to study appearances to endow them with a sense I'd lost. Therefore, I understood very early that the plausible doesn't coincide with the truth, or the real with its representation, something that quickly distanced me from my times. I also became isolated very early on because not only did I have to keep the secret of my loss of a sense of smell, but from people whom I didn't like very much since I could fool them so easily.

Around the age of ten, I finally dared to reveal my handicap. "Enough with the nonsense already," retorted my mother. I stopped talking about it and developed my intellectual skills even more.

In grade school, I got my best composition marks by describing the souk of Marrakesh, its brilliant colors and intoxicating odors. The teacher read my paper in front of everybody and even passed it around in other classes. This was my first success in the world. It made me think deeply about literature and deception: I'd never been to Marrakesh and had no sense of smell.

Staphylococcus aureus: these eight syllables have fascinated me for a long time. I was more than a little proud of having caught something that turned out so difficult to spell and enjoyed the obscenity inherent in venturing so far from my usual vocabulary. It was like saying a swearword with total impunity. Or speaking a forbidden language. I even had the satisfaction of discovering in a dictionary that what had nearly killed me was sometimes referred to in French as the "king's disease."

I inferred from this that death was as extraordinary and mysterious as the name of my disease was long and complicated. I had to stick with it from then on. From that moment, all diseases with names of fewer than fifteen letters became so much *malarkey*. When my father was diagnosed with cancer, I wasn't at all anxious about the outcome, figuring that a word with only two syllables couldn't take him away; however, everybody around me was getting worried and I feared I was being insensitive.

But it shocked me when he was hospitalized for acute peritonitis; suddenly his death seemed terribly near, to the point that I felt faint in the room where he lay in bed — even though my father was out of danger and my mother was sitting on the edge of his bed, joking. He was begging us not to make him laugh: they'd just stitched up his belly, and the least spasm was torture. He suffered a lot and in silence.

My "golden" staphylococcus led to the only hospitalization I underwent during childhood. I was spared all the usual removals of tonsils, adenoids, and appendix. But it's because I've always refused to be butchered. At meals my mother loved telling how at the hospital in Tizi Ouzou, the midwife who was washing the blood and mucus from the delivery off me asked in a cheerful voice, "You want him cut?" As my mother says this, she bursts out laughing and repeats several times for everyone to hear, "You want him cut?" doubling over even more, as do her guests. No one dreams of explaining to me that they're talking about circumcision. Which doesn't change anything, since that misunderstanding was precisely what my mother thought was a riot. But I shuddered for years and years at the thought that you could decide the sex of children after birth and that it was thanks only to my mother's goodwill that I was a boy and not a girl. What if she'd said yes?

After my case of staphylococcus aureus, I never again fell sick — for nearly forty years, it seems. My life has been consistent with my constitution, or vice versa, despite various excesses — or because of them. I've never suffered from constipation or headaches; and I don't call being sick the other two times I had to be hospitalized: first for a double fracture of the jaw after being beat up in the subway and then when I completely ruptured my Achilles tendon, which happened during a badminton game shortly before my daughter was born.

The truth is that I don't remember a thing about my staphylococcus aureus. Or rather, I have no memories other than those fabricated by my parents, who very often portrayed this heroic event of my childhood as if it were one of the great scares of their life. Their version has never changed. Which is that you catch it by drinking stagnant water and that I must have gotten it by licking the window of the train that I had to take every Sunday evening to come back from my grandparents'. "You were always putting something in your mouth," maintains my mother.

About twenty-five years later I met a girl in a train I was taking back from Berlin; she was sleeping scrunched against the window of the compartment; as I walked down the aisle past her, her eyes opened and it was as if she were incorporating me into her dream: an instant later she was behind me, hanging on my every gesture, and for the next seven years loved me with a virulent passion that seized me by the throat the moment she threw her arms around my neck. Her name was Laurence, I guess because "Low Rinse," a kind of dirty water, isn't a first name. She also suffered from a skin disease.

When I realized that this encounter re-created, down to the slightest detail, what my parents had said about how I caught staphylococcus aureus, I burst out laughing. And immediately stopped despairing about a love that up until then had seemed overwhelming and fatal. The shock of love that characterized our encounter was in fact toxic shock.

Besides, hadn't I planned it? Shortly after we met, Laurence told me, "You appeal to me"; to which I replied, thinking I was being clever, "Who's peeling, Miss?"—calling her "Miss" because I had been speaking to her formally for quite some time. I'd get what I bargained for because seven years of torment were to follow, worse than those of Alceste with Célimène; or monstrous delights, the kind that come only with diseases, those ultimate expressions of life when it no longer has any other choice.

Our love's incubation period ended quite quickly. Because after a few marvelously feverish months, everything became worse. There was a kind of hostility in her toward me, contained at first, but to which she eventually gave in, as if swallowed up by it. She'd contradict me about everything, and we didn't agree on anything, except in bed. She extorted feelings out of me constantly but never loved me more than when I wasn't there; it was as if her love for me wanted to exist without me, and we were, like day and night, exasperated by their perpetual alternation. At the beginning of summer, I informed her that she wasn't the girl for me. Too many things led to conflicts between us, and what followed could only be disastrous; it didn't even have the elegance to be unpredictable. Laurence refused to listen. We were sitting on the steps of a church. She wanted to get married.

I kicked her out several times; each time she came back and I always gave in. I detested the weakness of character I felt every time I was with her. Even those nights I spent in others' beds propelled me back to her. But it was because nobody could come like she did. It was enough to graze her breasts for her entire body to start trembling. Her very blue eyes always turned to navy black, and just staring at them made me feel as if I were being sucked into an emptiness that was teaching me I was nothing, not even dust, not even a speck. To try to exist, I produced sperm, erections, turmoil ad infinitum. In vain. With her, love came as an immense accumulation of orgasms that I realized were turning me into a frantic, indeterminate being.

Every day, Laurence called to tell me to take care of myself, and in her mouth, that sign of affection sounded like a threat. She also had a certain way of saying "I love you" that signified she was enjoying her umpteenth lover, yet another affair; it wasn't jealousy, but it wasn't as if I was expecting that many promises, and neither was I asking her to humiliate me more and more openly. Few of my friends shook off her advances. As she endlessly repeated how much she loved me, she meticulously trampled on everything I held dear, and I watched my own self-betrayal as I bore the unbearable. "Your angst about death is killing me," I stubbornly tried to make her understand. So she'd announce loud and clear that she loved all men, just like the one I'd known before her who had whisperingly claimed the opposite, making me deal with the same denial. The same fear.

She acted as if she wanted to take over my role, and I saw her trying to make me her wife, based on the conventional notion that men behave like assholes. One day she even thought that she was growing a penis; it was a cyst, incredibly phallic in shape, and I advised her to go see a doctor. "You can never stand it when something good happens to me," she replied, closing her thighs. She waited a long time before seeing a specialist.

If I resisted her, it drove her mad. She suspected a tactic. Or that I had a psychological problem and needed to go get treatment. She had the solutions to my case. "You have to stop refusing life," she'd tell me.

"Don't take yourself for life," I'd retort. "The only thing I'm refusing is what you're making me experience."

"It's not my fault."

"It certainly is." And so on, for seven years.

What she'd do with language was the most stifling of all. She was full of words, the most grandiloquent all-purpose ones, which she tossed out without caring where they fell. She meant nothing that she said. She could say the opposite of what she thought, and act accordingly. It was even a principle. Orgasms took the place of thought. She wanted to take advantage of everything. "Taking advantage" was her favorite phrase. You have to take advantage. But loving, living, existing weren't taking advantage, as far as I was concerned; each verb had its own meaning. The world wasn't a cake that you'd better stuff yourself with before it was too late. What world? What cake? Despite her small breasts and her fragile hypersensitivity, I couldn't put up with her syntax. When she spoke, she was millions, and that was too big a crowd for me.

Every day she'd kick the television, which I'd ended up watching like a drunkard to avoid seeing or hearing anything. I didn't want my story to finish like Unrath's in *The Blue Angel*. The punishment she was looking for had nothing to do with me. The huge slap I gave her once brought me no pleasure. My ideal didn't involve becoming a pimp or a gigolo. From the rubble of my feelings, which had turned against me, I hoped only to manufacture some antibodies against her. It was a matter of survival, I believed, just as I'd had to battle the

26

infection that attacked me from the inside at the age of four, in order not to die.

I learned to hate — and then be disgusted by — myself. I went so far as to listen in on her telephone conversations in the hopes of discovering what I didn't understand about our story. Once, I ended up vomiting in the bathtub after hearing her talk about me. She was laughing coarsely. Almost every time, just after having hung up, she'd come to my study, which was located on the same floor, to bill and coo; and as if in slow motion, I'd see her approaching me with a smile, putting her arms around my neck, and telling me that she loved me. At that moment I knew what self-pity meant. Her male and female lovers weren't spared in her conversations any more than I was, and I got a kick out of the way she'd capitalize on her social authority over them: to each she'd offer herself, making him think he was the only one; it boosted all their egos in the same way. The way she expressed her misery would have moved me if I hadn't been the butt of it. I would have laughed at her lessons in morality if she hadn't believed in them herself. It was too much for me.

My decline got so bad that I didn't dare confide in anyone. My life was like a sterile room I couldn't leave anymore, where I went through the throes of death again and again. I was ashamed of myself. Accused myself of not knowing how to love or let myself be loved. I'd tremble when I saw her coming. Sharing the same air with her cut off mine. From then on I lived only in my persistent skin rashes or unmanageably tangled hair, the only places where I found refuge. I kept seeing her just as much, every night. But I'd stopped believing that inside the clenched fist behind her back was a speechless little girl desperately signaling with her arms. I was realizing that you couldn't make a deal with staphylococcus aureus.

A certain Anastasie-Louise, a name that is still my colorful way of referring to penicillin, came to ease my anguish. In the parc de Chatou she took my hand, and her joy, which came from Trinidad, immediately became an antidote to the French disease eating away at me. For me she was that moly plant said in *The Odyssey* to have protected Ulysses from the sexual power of Circe, the sorceress who transformed sailors landing on her island into swine. Joyce remembered it later, which led to Molly's character in *Ulysses;* in my case, this wasn't fiction.

Besides, names containing *i* have always been my lucky charms: Lili Kim, Valérie, Aurélie, Mélanie, Caroline, several Nathalies, Catherine, Birgitt, Corine . . . They've always bucked me up, and they're responsible for my not having given up on life. On the other hand, the three women with whom I've lived are Gaëlle, Fabienne, and Laurence. For me, love is also an affair of vowels.

Anastasie went back to her country. I was vaguely planning to join her when Laurence announced that she'd stopped taking the pill. Far from surprising, her decision seemed obvious. Penicillin had saved me, so wasn't it logical that my departure from the *sterile* room was being scheduled? I thought that happy days were finally on the way, and I gave up Anastasie. Laurence was pregnant. For perhaps the first time, I felt in harmony with her, as if a veil had been ripped away to restore her to me. Suddenly I was no longer a four-year-old man. At last I loved her unreservedly. The birth of the child brought uncommon joy. She had my eyes and my forehead.

Nine months later, Laurence informed me that we were breaking up. She'd had to become a mother to decide. "Now that we've had a child, I can leave you because I know I'll never lose you," she told me over the phone. The sentence still bores through me, like a mole shut up inside my body. "Every time I reached out, you only pulled back farther," I cried with panic into the receiver. "Which 'father' are you talking about?" she replied gently. The circle had closed. Now I believed that there was nothing authentic left in me.

So that's what it was: I'd caught staphylococcus aureus. And what was perhaps the most extraordinary thing about it was that Laurence perfectly played the role my disease had assigned her (though I'm sure I played the character I'd been destined to in her dream). I'd made a perfect choice in her, and without her I never would have delved into my own darkness. The ultimate result was that by having my child, Laurence had made sure that she would never be altogether absent from my life; and staphylococcus aureus is a pathogenic strain from which you never recover: nested in the folds of the organism, after the devastating work of antibiotics, the germs merely lie dormant, waiting to awaken under unpredictable circumstances.

If my parents had told me that I'd fallen ill in a completely different way, for example, by rolling in grass or swallowing pebbles, I don't doubt that I would have fallen in love with someone else, and certainly not in a train. Which doesn't at all change the fact that I had to relive what I'd repressed. Of all the reasons that claim to explain an unhappy love affair, the one about my staphylococcus aureus is the one I prefer. We think we consider everything, and we forget childhood diseases.

I needed several years to rediscover an appetite for living and to recover a freedom of thought and behavior. I had just turned forty. Since the age of twenty, I'd always said that my life wouldn't really start until I'd reached that age. Such a conviction kept me going and gave me an excuse for all my whims. It also prevented me from committing suicide — and perhaps even, quite simply, from dying. I hadn't been wrong: once past forty, I actually felt as if I'd started to live, as if everything that had come before had been a mandatory interlude.

Obviously, it was too late when I realized that it wasn't a question of any kind of forty, but of being "fortyish," which almost rhymes with "aureus," though it's really not yet the "golden" years. By forty, I'd stopped being rash and had learned to deal with the one I'd caught at four, as well. I'd come out of it cured and had ended up persuading myself that life would only exist for me after forty. Consequently, the limits of my world were a word composed of five letters. When I realized that my existence was structured by language, I continued to be devastated. I thought that if the disease of my childhood had been called "thirtyish," I wouldn't have waited to become forty to figure this out.

As for knowing which sense I lost in that battle, I think it was the sense of orientation, which fails me today, whereas I had no lack of it before falling passionately ill with Laurence. A report describing how the North Pole had just tipped on its axis to become located in the Ardennes didn't surprise me at all at the time. I didn't think it was an April Fool's joke for one second.

The child got sick the day after Laurence left; a year later, she had surgery for a urethra that was growing too large and threatening to ruin her kidneys. In the meantime, each month at Necker Hospital she had to undergo injections that burst the overly fragile veins of her arms, feet, or forehead until a few ounces of blood could finally be collected for analysis. She screamed while I held her hands and spoke to her nonstop. Once a tired, clumsy nurse wanted to cut her carotid artery to speed things up. We had to cause a scene to keep the woman from doing it.

Concerning that period of her life, the child knows only what her mother and I have told her. From time to time, she becomes curious and has to be reminded of what she went through and doesn't at all remember, although her memory hasn't forgotten anything about the experience of death she had at the time. When I think of what that can mean, I want to rip apart heaven and earth.

LIFE IN AUBERVILLIERS wouldn't last much longer. In response to an ad in the papers, my parents were more than happy to exchange their public housing apartment in a dreary suburb for three rooms in Paris — on rue Marbeuf, no less, which is practically next door to the Champs-Elysées.

This was how I came to the capital at the age of five, and I would never leave. From that time on, my memories belong to me. Sometimes I think about what would have happened if we'd stayed in Aubervilliers. It was an ad for real estate, as well, that played a part in deciding my fate.

My childhood unfolded in a small area bordered on the north by rue Pierre Charon, on the south by avenue

Montaigne, on the west by avenue Georges V, and on the east by the Champs-Elysées. I go for bread on rue de Renaissance; the post office is on rue de la Trémoille, which my mother pronounces "Trémouille"; the toy store adjoins rue Clément Marot; my school is nestled into rue Robert Estienne, which is, actually, a dead-end street. By some whim of the prefecture, everything from the sixteenth century comes together below my house, and I whinny every time I pass rue Bayard, imagining I'm the knight it was named for; only rue Marbeuf, which means "Cow Pond," has a crude name. However, it alone is worthy of its plaque because it was used to bring cattle to the watering place when the Champs-Elysées were actually fields.

Toward the end of the street, the place where Arsène Lupin used to live has become a bank. And in 1995, a bomb wounded several people right after my mother walked by with her arms full of shopping bags on her way back from the Prisunic on the Champs-Elysées.

We live in three rooms on the sixth floor, with no elevator. You get to our place by the service stairs, at the back of the courtyard. Each time you do, you have to pass in front of the space where the garbage is stacked. The place is never lit, and I imagine monsters waiting for me in the shadows. One evening, when I'm taking down the trash, a big sewer rat scampers in front of me. I chuck the bags of garbage and race away.

Our apartment is long and narrow. My brother and I are in the same bedroom at the end of a hallway, next to our parents'. We sleep in bunk beds, and I'm on the bottom. For a long time my brother pees in bed, right over my head.

A third of our room is taken up by the bathroom; a screen protects you from seeing anything, but not from noises.

French windows in each room open onto a balcony that overlooks the building courtyard from the sixth floor. Through the window in the stairwell that opens at midstory, about six feet down, you can leap onto a guardrail and spring up to catch hold of a rung of the balcony; the strength returning to your arms allows you to brace yourself against a cornice and, after having brought your leg over the balcony, end up at our place. Going in the other direction is more complicated because you have to let yourself slip into nothingness before touching down on the guardrail of the window, and at that moment it's impossible to see what you're doing.

When I'm confined to my room on Thursdays, or when I'm a teenager, I go out on the sly at night by "taking the balcony," trembling with fear in the dark but proud of overcoming it.

My parents throw a lot of parties. For a costume ball, my mother turns into an Oriental princess while my father dances with her as François I. There are always some friends at our place. One time, Max challenges my father to guess who's playing the drums in a piece he just put on the turntable. He's holding behind his back the album cover of the long-playing record he brought. As I sit cross-legged in front of a big sound system, my eyes try to pierce the mystery coming from the speakers. We all hold our breath. It lasts a long time. Suddenly my father's voice utters musingly, "It's Sam Woodyard on the right and Sonny Payne on the left." Our friends applaud. My mother swells with conceit. Max congratulates him. I'm proud of my father; at the same time, a vague foreboding creeps through me: where I expected there to be one name, there were two.

Max is my parents' best friend. He's very tall and wears flashy silk scarves around his neck and indisputably chic suits. Wherever he shows up, it's like the sun. Always on unemployment, he appears before prospective employers showily dressed, sometimes smoking a cigar, and he treats them like his subordinates. Those times that a boss, charmed by so much style and thinking he can control it, gets the nerve to hire Max to sell insurance or something else just as inspiring, things always end up in court.

I adore Max.

For a long time I imagined that he was my real father.

He's another one who has slept with my mother.

Max's great love is Monica. She looks like Louise Brooks and is little too. During a car accident, she goes through the windshield and ends up disfigured. For months on end, Max goes to see her at the hospital; she doesn't recognize him.

The last time I see Max, he's living with a giant with a plaster cast on one leg and hairy arms. They have a child together, whom Max names Boris, in honor of Boris Vian.

One afternoon, Max locks himself in his room, puts a pistol in his mouth, and fires it. My father keeps the suicide to himself for a long time.

MY BROTHER AND I spend all our school vacations in Saint-Germain-en-Laye, in the Yvelines, where our grandparents have finally moved into an apartment built on the edge of the forest. That's where I always see Didier, the caretakers' son. Together we race bikes, build huts, hunt toads. But one nice afternoon when he's on his bike, circling the little house where his parents live, he begins to scream and jump up and down, chased by little blue flames. His father rushes out and tries to grab hold of his son, who's writhing on the ground; he's slapping the boy's body everywhere, rolling him against the ground, and tries to rip off his clothing. Didier's mother watches with both hands pressed against her mouth. Everything happens very quickly. Didier dies on the way to the hospital. While passing in front of the open kitchen window, a draft must have enveloped him in gas escaping from the stove, where his mother was heating up dinner; his nylon shirt took care of the rest, we learn the next day. Shortly afterward, the caretakers move away. The whole building watches them leave. Didier's father's two hands are bandaged. For several months I look for the word *nylon* on my clothing labels.

Thursdays, after having inhaled my mother's bottle of nail polish remover to the point of dizziness, I often end up pouring the stuff on my hand and setting it on fire with a match. Then I shake my flaming hand in front of me as if I were sending signals. I also set little plastic soldiers on fire on the balcony; I watch them melt and shrivel into themselves until all that's left is a little charred pile.

A lot later, it would be another Didier who introduced me to the one I wanted to inflame as soon as I saw her, but she was the one who ended up consuming me.

One night, my parents bring home a man and two Swedish women — a blond and a brunette they've met at the Ascott Bar on rue Pierre 1er de Serbie, where they often go to listen to jazz. Wakened by the music and the peals of laughter coming from the living room, I slip onto the balcony in my pajamas and watch them through the slits in the shutter. My mother is holding the brunette's face in her hands, and her expression is absolutely over the top. I think they're kissing, but the shutter conceals them at the last moment and I strain my neck in vain. It's my first experience of a sex scene.

It's just as difficult to see what the others are doing, though they seem to be having a great time; my father is filling glasses with wine and changing the 45s on the record player, and jackets are piling up all over the carpet.

After an hour, I'm cold, and since nothing amazing is happening, I go back to bed. But noise and curiosity keep me from sleeping, despite the bolster that I press against my ears. So I get up and risk coming into the living room on the pretext of going to the toilet. I'm eleven. My appearance amuses everybody. They sit me down on the couch. My mother serves me a Gini Bitter Lemon Tonic. The man asks me what grade I'm in. My answer seems to delight him. He also says that I must be aware that I have incredible parents. Then everyone loses interest in me. My father is dancing with the blond. My mother is clucking about what the man is saying in her ear.

The brunette ends up leaving. I keep serving myself Gini. Suddenly my mother comes up with the idea that everyone take a shower. They're all thrilled by her suggestion, and they start removing their clothes. The man is the first to get naked, and his penis hangs limply be-

41

tween his thighs. He's very hairy. I've never before seen a man's penis. My mother flicks it with her fingertips as if it were a little bell and exclaims, "But it's so little!" She breaks into nervous laughter, interrupted by horsy snorts. The man laughs and mimes Tarzan hitting his chest. Taking my mother by the hand, he leads her toward the bathroom. My mother shouts, "Come on, everybody, let's head for the water!" Then her eyes abruptly settle on me as if seeing me for the first time. "Come on, Grégoire, under the shower, no excuses!" she enthuses. My father intervenes to suggest that maybe I don't have to. I avoid looking at him. "Whatever he wants," laughs my mother, who is already running into the hallway and shaking her feet in every direction to get rid of her dress.

Then my father and the blond disappear. I stay alone in the living room. I'd like to go back to bed, but since the bathroom is in my room, I stay on the couch, drinking Schweppes because there's no more Gini. From the hallway come noises of laughter and squirting water. Then I don't hear anything. I wait. It lasts a long time. I do nothing.

My father reappears first. He's carrying a suit and has to leave for work because he's on duty this Sunday. Behind him is the blond, wrapped in a bath towel. Her hair is all tangled. I don't dare ask where Mom is. My father gets his black briefcase at the entrance and slips on his raincoat. He tells me that I ought to go to bed. I obey.

Huddled in my bed, I listen for even the tiniest noise that could come through the wall from my parents' room, where I'm assuming my mother is with the other man. But I can't hear the slightest sound and am getting worried. I stay on the lookout, with my eyes open for a long time. Daylight is beginning to seep through the shutters. So I get up and creep back to the living room without a peep.

The blond is sleeping on the couch. She's snoring softly. The bath towel barely covers her. I pull it down very cautiously to uncover her heavy breasts, the crevices of her belly, sparse blond pubic hair, which surprises me. She doesn't move. I didn't think her body would be so flabby, which upsets and repels me. I don't know how long I stay examining that strange, slack mass, like a beached whale, hoping and dreading at the same time that the girl will wake up. I'd like to lie next to her and be taken in her arms, have her kiss me and let me touch her. I dare to graze her breasts one time. She doesn't react. For a moment I think she's pretending to sleep. Finally, I go to bed and fall asleep.

When I wake up, the house is silent. The man and the blond woman have left. My mother is suffering from a massive attack of hives that are making her face swell. She's wearing sunglasses and is staying in bed. All day she's in a bad mood.

Three days later, as she's draining a pot of macaroni in the sink, she says to me, "I hope you weren't shocked the other evening." I sense that she's embarrassed and answer nonchalantly. Reassured, my mother relaxes. She smiles. "The blond was pretty, wasn't she." Her tone is full of innuendo. I don't say anything. "Go tell your father this is ready," my mother suggests, not insisting on anything, while placing the macaroni on the kitchen table. It occurs to me that the blond was actually pretending to be asleep.

Of all the comics designed as innocent entertainment during my childhood, *Sleeping Beauty* had the strongest impression on me. In my room, I became Saint Gregory slaying the black queen, who had changed into a dragon. And later, I enthusiastically kissed the girls I encountered, imagining that I'd finally awaken them; but they weren't asleep at all, or else in another fairy tale, belonging to them. I didn't understand. I couldn't conceive that those to whom I was attracted weren't in a certain way asleep, even if it wasn't on the couch in the living room at rue Marbeuf.

"How awful!" exclaimed my father one day, when I suggested during an innocuous conversation in a restaurant that two women having sex was a lovely thing to see.

"It's repulsive," my mother chimed in. She was genuinely outraged. This is the day I learn that depravity can compete with morality.

During another meal in a restaurant, I tell my father that I love him. Right afterward I feel as if a weight has been lifted off me, as if I'd just paid back a debt. He seems less moved than I am by my admission. Opposite us, my mother bites her lip, and her mouth forms a sad, bitter crease.

THERE'S A PHOTO of my father, my brother, and I walking on a forest path. I must be six. It's a small black-and-white snapshot with scalloped edges. It has the feeling of a pleasurable November. My mother must be holding the camera because she's not in the photo. I have no memory of this walk. Nevertheless it's the most beautiful memory of my childhood I've manufactured for myself.

When my brother and I do something stupid and exasperate my mother, she hits us with my yellow plastic Zorro sword. Out of bravado we laugh under the blows, supporting each other, which makes my mother insane with rage. But each time she gets tired before we do, her wrist gets sore, and she finally gives in. Every time, when she leaves, I glare at my Zorro sword; the fact that it lets itself be used against me is a sign of disloyalty.

Sometimes my father has had enough of my brother and me messing around in our room. So he shouts through the wall, "That's enough, or I'll use one of you to hit the other." That's his expression. Since I'm the lighter one, I have no doubt that I'll be the one used as the club, and I worry for a long time about how to cause the least harm possible to my brother as I ram against him.

"They accuse me of breaking glasses, but I'm always the one who does the dishes," my mother says rebelliously from time to time.

She's five foot three, and when someone makes a remark about her size, she always retorts, "Maybe I am short, but wonderfully well proportioned." Which means that she's not only short, she's also way off.

On certain auspicious days, she's been known to climb onto the table and, brandishing her fist, declare, "And if there's only one left, it'll be me."

My father is an excellent cook. Every Sunday he does the shopping and prepares the meal. His specialty is sautéed rabbit. When he's in a good mood or satisfied with me, he ruffles my hair and calls me "my little bunny."

My mother found work at Béghin-Say, where she became the personal secretary of the director, Louis Merlin, who was also in charge of Europe numéro 1, a popular radio station at the time, where I would leave behind a very bad memory years later, after happening to work there and creating a lot of mayhem.

One day at work, my mother receives a phone call informing her that a car has just run over the old lady who took my brother and me to school. Drunk as usual, Madame Legal was, actually, stumbling before our very eyes while ill-advisedly wanting us to cross as soon as the light turned green. A car brushed past her so closely that she collapsed into a puddle, more inert than wounded. My mother immediately quit her job to look after us. By doing so, she was giving up a promising position the likes of which she'd never be able to find again. "My children come before everything," she said with conviction.

Restless, unruly, undisciplined . . . these terms followed me during all my school years, at the same time as comments about my being "a good student" or "gifted student." I'm never bored. One Thursday afternoon, I invite home Leray, Fritère, and Gravet, three older pupils from school who are that much more inseparable because each is the son of a concierge. In my room, they have a field day with my stuff and navigate by elbowing me in the back, as if being let upstairs for once was giving them the opportunity to get even. That day, I realize that I wouldn't like to be the son of a concierge, if I had to be like them. They themselves must hate being a concierge's son, it suddenly occurs to me. Still, I find their envy of my lot an exaggeration, and I feel scorn for their scorn. Among us I've just discovered a world that doesn't belong to us and makes people bitter; instinctively, I refuse to submit to it, and even today no one can say he's my enemy without my consent.

That evening, my mother calls me into the living room. A hundred-franc bill has disappeared from its place on the mantelpiece. Her eyes are searching my pockets. She ends up sending me to bed and advising me to give some serious thought to it.

Two days later, Leray is playing in the courtyard of my building with a brand new BB gun. I dash downstairs. Leray denies having stolen the money. By his side, Gravet and Fritère back him up. I warn them that my parents already know the truth and that they're going to see Leray's father, maybe the police, probably the army. I make a point of warning him, since we're such good friends. Leray's ears are all red. He ends up giving me the BB gun and the rest of the money in exchange for my promise that I'll try to fix things with my parents. As I go back up, I feel very proud of myself and the way I strategized, given the situation.

When my mother gets home, I triumphantly hand over the loot taken from the enemy. She says, "I'm happy you're giving back the money, but don't let me catch you stealing again." I try to protest, but my intensity itself supports my mother's belief in my guilt. I end up falling silent.

From that moment on, I stop telling her anything else; she is no longer my mother, even if I still am her son.

MARIE-BLANCHE IS the younger sister of Fabrice, my best friend. To see them, you wouldn't think they were brother and sister because she is so delicate and radiant, with a slightly square face, whereas he's tall and lanky, blond and hairy. Marie-Blanche also has a small scar on her chin, and just thinking about it still slays me.

Marie-Blanche and I try to get a glimpse of each other through the bars of the little gate that separates the girls' school playground from the boys'. We exchange a few words. In the yard where the students from both schools gather once a week to rehearse the end-of-year show, we sing "L'Hymne à la joie" with our eyes locked on each other until they're misty with tears. After I get back to class, I keep thinking about her for a long time. When our parents run into each other, they joke, "Those two will get married one day." They don't know that we've already secretly pledged ourselves to each other.

I remember nothing but his family name: Delambre. One morning he comes to school with a steel marble that he swiped from his father's desk. No one has ever seen such a magnificent marble, and everyone wants to look at it, hold it in his hand.

It wins Delambre a prestige that I find exasperating. Somebody who was nothing in school, was a no-account and had no talent, suddenly becomes an important figure. Even my friends court him and find qualities in him that they thought he hadn't had the day before. So, a steel marble can change people's minds? Modify the face of the world? Invent a hierarchy where value depends only on what you possess? My disgust for the world of marketing dates to this incident.

For two days I pressure Delambre to shoot a game of marbles with me, using his steel one. He snivels that his father will cuss him out if he notices that the marble is missing. I make fun of his cowardice in front of the others. By turns, I hold out the prospect of a spectacular gain if he wins, boost our friendship in private, minimize the threat of his father, belittle my marble-shooting skills, and exaggerate his; and then once again I shame him in public, to deflate him. There's nothing I wouldn't do to convince him, except for physical violence, since for me it's not a matter of who keeps the marble but of knowing who's worthy of it.

All my marbles as well as the bag. Just one three-step shot. If I score, I win the steel marble. If not, I lose everything. No second match. The lure of gain has finally made up Delambre's mind. The match is set for lunch break. Everyone in school is informed. Fabrice tells me that I'm crazy; I could lose everything. I couldn't care less. The steel marble is for Marie-Blanche. I'm going to win.

The students gather around to hide us from the teacher who's watching the yard. We're behind the lavatories where the asphalt slopes gently down toward a small cement wall. The clock just sounded. Those who don't eat in the cafeteria begin to pour in and fill out the ranks. I'm worried that the teacher will intervene. Delambre won't give me another opportunity. Showing that he was capable of risking the marble will be enough for him to pull out of this affair. I won't have a second chance.

Ten feet away, against the wall of the lavatories, glitters the steel marble. I'm very calm. Concentrating more than I ever have. I feel as if nothing escapes my lucidity. I position my lucky marble—an old, dull clay one that, it has been agreed, I can keep if I lose. When Fabrice looms up next to me. He's coming back from lunch at his place and wants to speak to me. I tell him that this isn't the time. He insists. He has a secret to tell me. I tell him to get lost. Later. I don't even look at him. All I see are my marble and the shiny steel one over there. I can feel the energy of the crowd above my head. I release my index finger. My marble takes off in a perfectly straight line. It zooms exactly where I want it to go, as if magnetized, I already know I've won, it's obvious, I've won, when Fabrice suddenly gets in front of me and kicks my marble, dispersing in one blow all the heaven of my childhood.

Did I cry out? I really don't know. Fabrice is lying flat, and I don't understand what he's doing on the ground. He isn't moving. His body is weirdly twisted. His hair is spattered with blood. The entire school makes a circle around me and stares at me without moving. It's like an immense wall keeping me at a respectful distance. Every eye is glued to me. What do they want from me? They're like statues. Not one of them makes any kind of gesture or does anything. I don't recognize anybody. See nothing but the colors of the clothing. Lots of colors. I don't know where to look. The sky is blue. What's wrong? There's an amazing silence in the courtyard, I suddenly realize. No noise anywhere. Not a scream. Total silence. As if all of life had been interrupted. It occurs to me that this quiet isn't normal. I remain standing without moving. I wish I wasn't there anymore. I can feel something in my hand. It's a thick tuft of hair with a shred of very white flesh hanging from it. Fabrice's scalp. My hand is refusing to open. I can't move it. What have I done? Marie-Blanche. I start shaking. All my limbs are clattering. I can't stop shaking.

It's a teacher who pulls me out of the circle. He drags me by the collar onto the playground, where he makes me stand in the corner with my hands on my head, in front of the pile of mats. He leaves. I stare at the blue color of the mats. Think of nothing. I concentrate only on the blue pigmentation of the foam rubber, to which I'd never paid attention and which suddenly seems like a fantastic material. The end of one of the mats has been torn off, as if someone had bitten into it with relish.

I stay on the playground for a long time. Everyone has gone to class quite a while ago. I figure my brother must have seen me earlier in the yard. I hear an ambulance siren. Then it disappears. Then a noise. I remain alone. The playground is gigantic. No one comes. I get rid of the tuft of hair I'm holding in my hand by sticking it between the mats. I avoid looking at it.

Another teacher comes to get me. He says, "Where are your things? Your mother's coming to get you." We go to get my schoolbag in the courtyard. I don't dare ask him about Fabrice. Next to the lavatories, I can see my lucky marble in a corner. I don't pick it up. A baffling period of time separates me from it now.

In his office, the principal leaves me standing. He stares at me and says, "I hope you're proud of yourself!" Then he examines a beige form on which I recognize my I.D. photo. Without raising his eyes, he says, "So, would you do things like that in your country, in Tizi Ouzou?" He says "Tizi Zouzou." He also says, "And of all people, the Fenwick boy. You're finished, young fellow." I think I understand that my parents could have some problems with Fabrice's family. I hang my head.

My mother arrives, all out of breath. Her face is stern. The principal has her sit down on a chair and orders me to stand in the corner in the hallway. When my mother comes out of the principal's office, all she says is "I hope you're proud of yourself."

In the street, she walks fast, and I'm ten feet behind her. When we get home, she makes me kneel on the edge of her bed, pulls down my pants, and lashes me with my yellow Zorro sword. When her arm is tired, she leaves. I remain in that position all afternoon. My mother comes from time to time to get something in her room and spanks me as she goes by. This lasts until nightfall.

Later, I hear her on the telephone. "A boy thing . . . that's what it is . . . nothing serious . . ." She's talking to Fabrice's mother. She says "Madame Fenwick" deferentially. I realize that Fabrice has gotten stitches. I don't know what stitches are, but this must be a good sign. Which doesn't at all change my feeling about having killed him. About having killed.

On the telephone, my mother describes what happened in the courtyard as if she had been there. From the tone of her voice I sense that she's relieved about the way the conversation is going. She even laughs before hanging up. What's so funny? And then, why punish me? But I couldn't care less. I deserved a whipping, yes, she could have even hit harder, that's nothing compared with what's got me in its grip, like a horrible fear that has just opened a pool of nothingness in me. What's happened to me? Where did this violence come from? In the darkness, these questions torture me. But no matter how much I try, I can't remember anything. There's a gap in my timetable that now separates me from myself. A gulf into which I've disappeared and come out as someone else. I feel as if my body has betrayed me. I can't trust it anymore. I tell myself that I'll have to keep an eye on myself. Yes, from now on I need to be wary of myself. And especially my right hand. That's the one that scalped Fabrice. Not me. I have nothing in common with that hand.

A lot later, I remember having planned to cut it off with the electric knife used to slice meat for Sunday lunch. I spend a long time pushing the teeth of the blade into my wrist, my finger ready to switch it on. But I tell myself that the pain will be so great that it will be impossible for me to cut all the way through. I finally give up.

I'm suspended from school for three days. I have no memory of returning to class. I only know that Fabrice and I remain friends despite what happened. Throughout the whole school I now enjoy a reputation that no one even dares to challenge. I hide from everyone the fact that it's built on a void.

Today there's still a marble at the bottom of my pocket. It rolls in my hand each time I take out some change to pay. Also, for years I've frequented a bar in Montparnasse; I hadn't realized it was located on rue Delambre. This is the place where I've often gone in search of oblivion, with people who, like me, seemed to have lost all their marbles.

A year later, I'm playing with my pal Bruno in the schoolyard when my brother comes up to me: he wants to talk to me. It seems important. I leave Bruno on the spot to follow him, even leap to my feet; but Bruno wants to hear what we're saying, trails behind us laughingly, and refuses to leave us alone. He doesn't understand that I'm not joking, so I chuck a little iron car right at his head. He falls backward. His face is covered with blood. His eye is nearly punctured. I turn to stone and stay that way. I'm not shaking or anything. I'm only surprised by the uncanny precision of my throw. Even though Bruno was a good ten feet away, I didn't miss. Just as I wouldn't have missed the steel marble.

Once again I'm suspended from school for three days. I laugh it off. I merely suppose that I must be cursed: whatever I do, things end badly. This time, however, I was careful not to reproduce my error of last year: I'd actually stopped playing to hear what was being said to me, I'd done everything correctly so that I wouldn't find myself in the same situation. To no avail. What's wrong with me? Can't it be changed? Not to mention that for the second time I never found out what there was to tell me that was so important.

One night our parents have just turned off the light in our room when my brother leans down from his bed and calls to me in the dark, "Grégoire, I have a secret to tell you." Immediately I climb the ladder between our bunk beds and join him in his bed. I wait for him to speak. But instead of that, he begins feeling me up in the darkness and kissing me. I don't understand what he's up to. His hand is pulling at my pee-pee. His other hand is guiding me toward his groin. I feel hairs and his busy fingers. I don't move. My brother is breathing heavily. When he's finished, I climb back down into bed and go to sleep.

To this day, I no longer have any memory of the two of us speaking to each other like brothers.

MY MOTHER ALWAYS PREFERRED me to my brother. She refused to admit it for a long time, but everyone knew it,
which was a problem for each of us, though for different
reasons. One day when my brother and I were playing
on the balcony, my mother heard me say, "You wouldn't
be able to jump." She rushed out in time.

On that same balcony, my brother hits his nose hard
against the window ledge. The result is an enormous
black eye that takes over his whole nose and both eyes.
The next day, my parents are called in by the school principal. My brother has pretended that my father beat him.

When he's a teenager, my brother invents a game: he
glides silently behind my mother while she's busy and
stays there without moving or breathing, for example,

while she's rinsing salad in the sink; each time she turns around, she comes out with a loud shriek, jumps, and puts her hand to her heart. Sometimes my brother waits for her behind a door. He moves throughout the house without making the slightest sound. Like an Indian or a ghost. This little game lasts several months. My mother no longer does anything without being on the alert, fearing she'll discover her son suddenly looming before her like a silent reproach. An unfulfilled claim.

One Christmas, while the whole family is opening presents, my brother piles his into a corner and says, "I'll open them tomorrow." Then he goes to bed.

My brother was sent to the United States. Under threat of repeating a year at school for the second time in a row, unhappy at home, he needed a change of air, my parents thought; and he did really seem to be suffocating in France—but only he knew why. He spent a year with a Texan family and came back with bleached hair. When my parents were pulling together the money needed to send him, they informed me that this was a sacrifice we all had to make.

His return to us was disastrous. For whole months he stayed in bed, his arms at his side, stiff and unmoving, doing and saying nothing, staring at the ceiling. It was the horizontal version of that ghost who had loomed insidiously behind my mother a year ago, but now he expected nothing of her. I'd leave him in that position in the morning and find him the same when I came home from school. Encountering nothing but a wall in him, my parents became exasperated. Evenings, my brother would disappear to join a writer who was giving him an education that was more sexual than literary. In any case, he hardly read. My parents, on the other hand, devoured mysteries.

My brother looked forward impatiently to one thing only: going back to the United States. He did his military service, then worked as a salesclerk at Roissy airport to pay for his plane ticket. Lacking money, he traveled across the United States by prostituting himself. "It's ridiculous how many fathers of families are fags," he confided in me when, years later, I went to see him overseas.

Finally he moved to San Francisco and never came back to live in France, sending practically no news for ten years. At first my mother frantically tried to find out if her son was homosexual or not, which upset her more than it did my father. "I knew it. Even when he was very young he preferred boys," she proclaimed, after having forced my brother's best friend to reveal the truth.

Although my brother was able to live as a homosexual without any obstacles in San Francisco, he nevertheless remained on the margins of the gay community, playing the role of provocateur. "I'm a repressed hetero," he posted above his bed.

During the day he sold CDs and at night was a disc jockey in clubs. He was like an eternal adolescent. Raised hell in every way and laughed it off as if he were acting in an endless comedy. He wasn't thirty, but twenty plus ten: after a first life in French, he lived a second in English, and these two existences never seemed to coincide in him; they were even exclusive of each other. If he had sought to become himself, I think he was only half of it standing in for the whole, and his solution didn't convince me.

I still hear his voice telling me, "When I found out I had AIDS, I was relieved." He didn't say about what.

Before dying, he came back to France to say goodbye to the whole family; despite the ocean he'd put between it and himself, he seemed more attached to it than me.

He was in appalling shape. My father and mother took care of him. One day he asked them to forgive him. Yet again without being any more precise. Then he went back to the United States, where his lover took care of him until the end.

The day before he died, I spoke to him on the telephone. His birthday was the next day. I remember thinking that if he made it past his birthday, he'd be able to put off the date of his death for a year. He just needed to hold on for twenty-four hours to have one more go-around of existence, until the next time. Because there's a temptation to go out where you came in, to take the same rift in time through which your soul, to use the common parlance, has to become incarnate in a body. Ludwig Wittgenstein died on April 29 and was born on April 26, whereas Thomas Bernhard passed away two days before celebrating his fifty-eighth birthday, which is also the anniversary of the death of his grandfather, whom he adored; the river into which Osamu Dazai threw himself washed him back up on the very day of his thirty-ninth birthday; and there were so many others, famous and anonymous, who attempted to close the parentheses at the place where they had opened. My brother didn't have the strength to go by square one a thirty-third time; he died during the night.

Before he hung up, I told him I loved him. I wasn't thinking a word of it. Not that; or that way, in any case. It was to please him. I had the impression that he wanted me to make a concession of that sort for him. Everything unfolded for us as if we were acting out the end of a film, maybe because that opportunely rendered unreal the end of his life. But that said, I had the vague feeling that I was coming to pronounce his sentence and hasten his leaving. Making that avowal to him was saying farewell, giving him permission to go, maybe encouraging him to. While he was alive, I'd never made such a statement. After I hung up, I remained looking at the telephone for several minutes. I knew that I'd just heard his voice for the last time. The next day he was dead.

IT'S WINTER, and it's night when my brother and I come back from school one evening after study period. The apartment is strangely dark. My mother is crying in the living room. Hearing us, she turns on the little light on the mantelpiece. She's sitting in the big Henri II chair. Her eyes are red and swollen. We look at her silently. Finally she says in one breath, "Children, your father has left. He wants a divorce. Who do you want to go with?" I stand there stupidly, watching my brother rush toward my mother, hug her, kiss her everywhere; it's as if he's always been waiting for this moment, and his eagerness sickens me. My mother dissolves into tears. She's pressed against him too. They stay with their arms around each other, as if they've melted.

I don't move. I'm stock-still in the middle of the living room. At my feet my schoolbag remains standing on its own. I'm looking toward the entryway. I stare at the big bottle-green velvet curtain that covers the door, and it's as if I were waiting for a response from it that isn't coming. It's the last thing to have seen my father, and I have the impression that it would be enough for me to raise it to see Dad appear in front of me. He hasn't abandoned me. It isn't possible. What did I do? I want to go with him. But she couldn't stand it. She's going to throw herself out the window again, or I don't know what, if I don't answer right. I don't want her to kill herself because of me. This time there won't be anyone to catch her.

I hate her for asking us that question. She has no right. I refuse. This is the only thought running through me. But I lower my head and hear myself murmur very quietly, "With you, Mom." Then I clearly hear the sound of a sheet tearing. A totally incongruous sound. What is it? I turn my head. But it's coming from me. Yes. It's in me. Inside me: a sheet is tearing in my body. I hear it distinctly. It's even quite loud. It definitely is a sheet. Something is tearing in me that is a sheet. You'd say it was coming from my belly or my chest. I don't have the time to discover more about it before it's over. Two or three seconds at the most. Then, there's a sheet inside

68

me? My mother dries her tears. She says, "Thank you, children. How nice." I hate myself.

Even today I know of nothing that can tear you up as much as a sheet.

One day my daughter looked at a photo of her mother and me when we were together, and she had that mute, inconsolable look of those who know that their happiness, whatever they do, will hereafter be based on a misfortune that isn't even theirs, and that has stricken them unjustly, by surprise. I would have given anything not to rediscover that look on my child's face. For putting me in that position, I nearly killed her mother. She was never even aware of it. But actually, she'd dreamt that her own mother was leaving her father.

When I earned my first salary at sixteen, I bought a four-track Akai tape recorder; I see myself for one whole day busy recording the sound of a sheet tearing and a door closing. The idea came to me without my knowing how. I'm not asking myself that question. I just want to make music, and since I don't know how to play any instrument, I work with what I have at hand.

But the tape recorder doesn't succeed in reproducing what's in my head. This isn't my sheet that's tearing, nor my door slamming. Whether I send the door hurling or close it crisply, rend the sheet with a brief movement or very slowly, the sounds that come back to me through the tape remain approximations. Nevertheless, I keep at it, fascinated by my device's trick. I feel as if I'm gliding along in another time. It's a new experience. For once I'm not the problem; the mike is.

Finally, I manage to make a mix that creates the illusion. It's the best piece of music ever recorded because I've put the best of myself into it. The slamming of the door provides the rhythm, and the tearing sheets play the melody. You'd say it was riffs from an electric guitar. Sometimes an organ in a cathedral. The piece lasts eight minutes. I call it "A Fine Pile of Sheet." It exudes a harsh, repetitive harmony that moves me. Something African and futuristic at the same time, including a middle passage that expands time to the point of silence. I have to listen to it a billion times. Never have I heard stuff that was similar. It's something I've invented. I play it for my friends. They think it sucks. They want to hear the latest Rolling Stones. They'd rather play Marcel Dadi sheet music and smoke joints.

A year later, my father comes back home. I don't know how it could be possible: suddenly he's there. But it's not him. It's another man, sporting a beard. My father never wore a beard. It's somebody pretending to be him. I haven't had a father for a year. I don't want one anymore. My father left a year ago. Mom said so. She would have told us if he'd come back. We would've known. You don't come back once you've left. All this pain for nothing. That would be laughable.

That summer at my grandparents, I read *Le Trésor de Rackham le Rouge.* It's the Tintin comic book in which Professor Sunflower appears. He comes to knock on Tintin's door to offer him a submersible that he has invented. When I read that page, I'm shocked. That little bearded man, wearing a hat and glasses who appears at the door dressed in green gabardine down to his feet, yes, just as I immediately suspected: it's a disguise. He's not who he pretends to be.

Hergé always claimed that his inspiration for the character of Sunflower was the Swiss physician Auguste Piccard, whose photos show that he actually resembles Hergé's character, but without the beard! In reality, if you strip Sunflower of everything he's hiding under (as well as Hergé's words), you discover the face of Rackham the Red, the despicable pirate said to have disappeared three centuries before in the explosion of his ship, *The Unicorn.* You can tell: his pointed beard gives him away. Sunflower is actually a phantom. If he's deaf,

71

it's because his eardrums couldn't withstand the explosion of *The Unicorn;* from now on he's called Sunflower; which pretty much puts him back in the light of day; and the submersible he's offering is shaped like a shark, not to say a fluke, and something about it certainly is "fishy." So, three centuries later, the pirate is back, but incognito. It really is him, just as my father really is mine after twelve months of absence. Except for the fact that the cruel crook has been transformed into an inoffensive professor; and that summer, I can't stop wondering what could really have happened between the two comic books to make my father, that phantom, seem so different and unrecognizable.

When I reveal this discovery to my mother one day, she looks at me, dumbfounded. "But your father had that beard a long time before all this happened," she protests. "In fact, I was the one who made him grow it right after our marriage since he was so ugly with his receding chin. Your memory's playing tricks on you, son." I'm instantly taken aback. I was persuaded that my memories couldn't lie or invent anything. Not mine. Only they show what happened. And yet they too are betraying me. Like everything else.

HER NAME WAS EVE — to each his mythologies — and she's the reason why my father left home. Having become director of the grocery section of a Monoprix store, he'd begun to make money for the first time in his life — and obviously figured that he then had what it takes to fall in love. Because he was consumed by an extravagant passion, and because he blew all his money on escapades with Eve and presents for her, including money he didn't have, bills started arriving at my mother's. Then jewelers lodged a complaint for bounced checks. It was for a lot of money, compared with what my parents earned. The affair went so far that my father risked going to jail. Eve found the optimum moment to realize that she didn't love my father anymore. He came back to his wife and children.

My mother hired a lawyer and planned my father's defense so well that he got out of going to jail. Blacklisted by the Bank of France, he was prohibited from having an account for ten years. And he had to pay back the charges for his adulterous generosity, which took several years.

My mother may have agreed to take her husband back, but she didn't forgive his having told her one day that he could have had children with anybody; from then on, she refused to let him touch her. It was the beginning of an endless series of arguments. My mother provoked my father endlessly, and she knew how to torture him; he'd always end up exploding. During a Monopoly game, she ticked him off to such a degree that he threw a large glass ashtray at her head; the ashtray just missed it, and the big living room window behind her shattered. What if it had hit her? "You poor buffoon," my mother came out with, contemptuously.

When we'd watch television, the air in the room would freeze the moment a couple kissed on the screen.

I slept with earplugs so that I'd stop hearing them.

Parties with dancing and laughing friends ended; they disappeared one by one.

It was in that warm atmosphere that I went through adolescence. Every second was a huge ball of violence, dominating the living room; you had to hug the walls to avoid touching it and causing it to explode.

Every morning, I'm glad to go to school. After class, I get into the habit of hanging out in the street. I shoplift. Then dump my thefts in the gutter. I also break open car doors in the parking lot on avenue Marceau. Break windshields with a hard chestnut. Sometimes my mother comes to get me at the police station. She never bawls me out in front of the officers.

One evening when I come home late yet again for dinner, from the stairwell I can hear my parents arguing. I ring reluctantly; my father opens the door and sends a fist flying into my face as he says, "When are you going to stop making your mother worry!" I get back up and dash into my room.

My mother comes to see me later. "Your father didn't mean to hurt you. He's in a real state now. You ought to go hug him."

My mother only softened up the day my father was diagnosed with testicular cancer at age forty, exactly one year after his acute peritonitis. The fear that the man she'd fallen in love with at sixteen would die finally rendered her compassionate. One appendix and one ball less were obviously enough to make her think he'd been punished already. My father got radiation therapy. Little blue dots like tattoos appeared almost everywhere on his body.

When we had first moved to the rue Marbeuf, my parents had hung in the bathroom a series of photos representing the seven capital sins. They were large, attractive color prints on shiny paper. Each sin was depicted conceptually, as if these were advertisements for theft or murder. Over the course of years, the photos came unstuck from the wall and disappeared one by one. Except for two, which held out with stubborn resistance, for I don't know how long: sloth (a man with a straw hat stretched out in the sun) and anger (a fractured windowpane on a blood-red background). At times I think that this wasn't by chance.

On the throne, I manage not to make a sound that could be heard through the door and expose me to the ears of the world. I cough at the moment of the classic plop! Once, I dream about fitting out a shelter in some obscure corner. I see myself living there away from harm, protected from everything, never having to leave because I can relieve myself right there. This practical aspect delights me. Through a window shaped like a porthole, a rope would bring me food.

One day, I take advantage of my parents' absence to watch television in their bedroom on the sly. I'm hoping to catch anything at all that's forbidden and exciting, which is indicated at the time by a white square. But instead I happen upon Max, disguised as a musician, except that he's wearing pigtails and his hand, made of modeling clay, is changing into a thousand fingers, coming to life over the neck of an electric guitar. At one point he says, "When I was a kid, every time I met a girl, it never happened like it does in songs. I've never written a love song. You shouldn't lie to kids."

A few years later, I'll find out that it's Frank Zappa. Among all the idols that were already being marketed for young people, to steal their youth and age them as quickly as possible, he was the only one I admired for his refusal to be an idol, though he had more talent than most of them. He was the spirit of laughter, just as Lautréamont was the one who first introduced me to poetry. Originally, his group was called the Motherfuckers—how could he have known about me?

Nobody but he knew how to put together a piece based on a single note, the way you pass the ball with your foot during rugby to make a successful hole in the line of attack. With him, borders revealed their annoying intention of separating things and beings. Freedom, pleasure, invention: everything my life lacked I could hear in his music. I wanted to live in such a world, which would finally give existence some panache, but I was fed up with finding it only within the grooves of a record.

AGE NINE. I'm in the immense foyer of the Fenwicks' apartment, and Marie-Blanche and I are supposed to hide while Fabrice counts to a hundred. We separate, and soon I am lost in rooms that appear in endless succession, hallways opening on a small living room, then a spacious office, then another small living room—and still not the slightest hint of a bedroom.

The blue wall-to-wall carpeting is so thick that I don't hear myself walk. There are paintings everywhere, flowers in vases, big windows with little different-colored panes halfway up, looking out onto the park surrounded by the traffic circle at the Champs-Elysées. It's a fantastic maze, a thousand times bigger than rue Marbeuf. But after a moment the heavy silence around me makes me nervous. I'd like to find the others and get out of this hushed labyrinth, for which I lack any directions. But I can't figure out where I am. I go in circles and get upset about not going anywhere.

At the end of a hallway I push open a door. A bathroom. Her back to me, Madame Fenwick is washing her bottom in the bidet. She's naked. What a dazzling sight. I've never seen anything so beautiful.

Today I'm still grateful that Madame Fenwick didn't hear me coming because I was able to watch her in comfort for a few lengthy seconds. I don't even think of hiding. Full of admiration, I remain in the doorway of the bathroom, careful only not to disturb the perfection of that scene, which I'll be able to match to a thousand faces, because it insists on none in particular. Imprinted in my memory is only the vision of a radiant back, the auburn loveliness of hair caressing shoulders, the golden undulation of a spine while the arm bends to disappear between the thighs, followed by the hollowing of the small of the back as the washcloth slides into the parting of buttocks — Ingres and Delacroix reconciled in a bathroom, just for me.

I'm hot. A heat with which I'm totally unfamiliar. My heart is beating crazily. I can even hear it getting closer. But those are steps in the hallway! When I turn around, Fabrice's grandmother is standing in front of me. She looks me up and down with an attitude that makes everything in its wake turn dirty. In her eyes I read a wrong that she's attaching to my eyes, making me own, and suddenly I'm nothing but a worm. I've been condemned out of hand. Everything is testifying against me. I flee at a run, pursued by that vile glance, as if my hurrying could shake it off.

When I find Fabrice, I don't dare say what happened. After all, it's his mother. My nerves are in bad shape. Madame Fenwick must already have been informed about what kind of little pervert I am. I wish I'd never been born. I'm just as terrified at the idea of running into that horrible witch who ruined everything. Yet again, everything ruined. Ruined at the last moment. At the best moment.

Marie-Blanche is back with us, and suddenly I feel like a stranger in her presence. But there's no time to think about it. Nor about that peculiar triangle made up of the woman, the girl, and the old lady, and whose geometry, without my knowing it, is already beginning to weave the web of my imagination. Urgently I suggest we all go play in the park in the Champs-Elysées. However, Fabrice needs to ask his mother's permission. Soon she comes into the main living room. I make myself as inconspicuous as possible in a corner.

She's fantastic, with a style that I'll eventually learn belongs only to women when they're totally fulfilled and have never had to wash a dish in their life. Only the refined bourgeoisie sometimes produces such fabulous specimens, which is its sole, yet demoralizing, merit.

Madame Fenwick is wearing a dove-gray blouse. You can see her breasts through it, and I catch myself looking at them out of the corner of my eyes. Obviously, I'm not the boy I was. I'm ashamed, but everything is intense. It has left me with an exaggerated taste for blouses and necklines, on any woman at all.

Madame Fenwick has come up to us, and Fabrice is asking her if we can go out. While he's speaking, I get the nerve to raise my eyes and look at her. I'm resigned in advance to the inevitable. But above Fabrice's shoulder, Madame Fenwick sends me a smile that's for me alone, which saves me for the rest of my life. A pixie's smile. What I owe such a smile can't be measured. It tells me that I'm not to blame, nothing is ever lost, beauty is a source of goodness, existence bliss, the unexpected the only approbation of life, and so much more, about which Madame Fenwick couldn't have any idea, but which refutes the fate that society and my family are already reserving for me. I wish everybody could meet a Madame Fenwick someday. Especially since she's suggesting that I stay for lunch and join them for a game of golf that will take all of us outside Paris for the afternoon. I don't know what golf is, but it must be heavenly. Never have I been so happy.

On the telephone, my mother doesn't make it too difficult to get permission for this impromptu Sunday outing. In the thickets of the park in the Champs-Elysées, where Fabrice, Marie-Blanche, and I have gone to play, I gambol about like a lamb, and my strength seems limitless. I could straddle the entire city.

When we go back to avenue Gabriel, Madame Fenwick is sitting in one of the big chairs in the living room. She's crying. Standing next to her, her mother is patting her shoulder, but without conviction, as if all consolation was useless. I don't understand. I have the impression of already having lived this scene, but for the moment I don't know where. What happened? Earlier she was smiling, and now . . . I'm aware that the situation has reversed, but I can't interpret it.

The party is over. Once more I stay in the doorway, always in the doorway, of the living room or the bathroom, as if in front of a screen, the scene appearing before me at the eleven-o'clock position, north by northwest, to be exact—and since that time I've never stopped walking in that direction: north by northwest, as if there were no other for me, to walk through the doorway, finally, go through the image, join Madame Fenwick, save her, yes, my steps always spontaneously lead me in that direction; even today, to buy bread I prefer the bakery that's at a north-northwesterly angle, even though its bread is always overbaked.

The party is over. I'd like to evaporate Madame Fenwick's tears. Do something. Anything. Erase this terrible painting that's altering the lustful Boucher of the bathroom. To think that an art form has disappeared while we played outside. I don't understand. I have only these two scenes to hang on to. They don't manage to coincide. They contradict each other, opening an abyss between them. I'm looking for a thread that leads from one to the other, doing my best to piece together a space of time, all the missing images that would lead from the bathroom to the living room, from joy to tears. In vain. And there I stay as if anesthetized, empty of life, without anything left to feel, neither emotion nor sensation, only the heavy need of nothingness, like fog invading me from behind my eyes, a nameless inertia with no temperature into whose thickness I'm dissolving, leaving only a statue of myself changed into stone, which must remain a fixture standing at the entrance, without anyone knowing it.

The party is over. That's all I'm sure of. Old lady Fenwick comes toward us to keep us from entering the room. Behind her, her daughter turns her head to hide from our eyes. She keeps lying there, this is much more than sorrow, it seems as if she'll never be able to get up, as if her existence had just collapsed at her feet and must never again see the light of day.

What is more, the entire room seems to have been plunged into utter despondency. The light, once radiant, is dismal. Old lady Fenwick tells me I have to go home. Of golf, no mention. I don't ask any questions, don't argue. Now I'm used to being disillusioned. The essence of life is beginning to penetrate me, forcefully. But how abrupt: I've barely had the time to say good-bye to Fabrice and Marie-Blanche when the door has already closed on me. Suddenly, on the landing, my life is no longer worth anything.

I don't know then that I've just seen the Fenwicks for the last time. Because I'll never again have the chance to go to avenue Gabriel, which is so aptly named, and where I received so many annunciations.

A moment later I'm walking toward the traffic circle at the Champs-Elysées. There's an enormous crowd, blocking traffic. Strangely, it's almost dark. People are shouting things I don't understand at all. Some of them are holding banners, or black or red flags. Others have hidden their face with a scarf or a sash. Commotion everywhere. I can see some of them throwing things at I don't know what target. Shouts of joy prolong the fall. Rushing in every direction, collisions, grunts. A girl gets hit in the face, keeps running on all fours.

I can't make sense of any of it. It's as if the world had totally changed the way it looked, in one afternoon. Everything is happening too fast. Swarming. Colliding. I feel tiny. One event follows on the heels of another, with no apparent link, no meaning that I can fathom. But I know that my own story has just been radically altered. The world isn't nine years old like I thought it was: this is 1969 and I'm not the center of anything. I'm nothing. Alone. The universe doesn't belong to me. There's a world that belongs to adults, and not the ones I know. Like a shifting of the scale in my disfavor. I don't feel part of anything. Contact was broken. I'm a stranger. Out of place. Free, empty.

In the middle of the street, I have to struggle not to be trampled. I'd like to go home. But sudden movements of the crowd force me along with the others. I'm running without knowing why. I'm afraid. I can hear nothing but the shortness of breath of the people bolting forward with me. It's like one gigantic animal respiration. I squeeze past the shadows as well as I can. It's exciting too. Again I start forging forward. Heading north by northwest.

When I feel myself lifted off the ground; behind his visor, a member of the riot squad is bellowing at me about what the hell I'm doing there. He's brandishing his billy club over my head. I run away as fast as my legs will carry me. Avenue Montaigne is open. I don't take another breath until I arrive at rue Marbeuf.

My father opens the door in his pajamas, and I tell him only that the golf game was canceled at the last moment. He goes back to sleep with my mother.

I spend all the rest of the afternoon in my room, locking into the deepest part of me every minute of that incredible day that aged me by two thousand years and revealed the incorruptible fullness of life. For the first time, I know that my life is my own. The events have given birth to my self to the power of ten, and I feel rich with an existence that owes nothing to anyone.

That evening, the whole family gets together to eat off trays in front of the television, while waiting for the Sunday evening movie. Everything takes place as if nothing had happened. As if I were still the same. Yet daily life has been smashed in two. How can the walls, the plates, the bedspread still remain in place? Doesn't anyone see that nothing can be as it was before? Even so, I've lived an entire life in one afternoon, and it's impossible that it could have happened unnoticed. There must be a mark on my face, a crease, something, a speck of the cosmos in my eyes. But no. Dad hands me a piece of bread. Mom wipes her lips before taking a swallow of red wine. I see every gesture, and each seems out of proportion. Their ridiculous repetition hits me in the face for the first time.

I'm trembling about it on my chair. I can't see them anymore. It's a trap. All of it's false. An outrageous lie. I saw. I didn't dream it. I know. Madame Fenwick and all the rest of it. There's another dimension. A time that is true to life. Wind. A magic that I don't want to forget. That's it: magic. I mustn't forget it. Ever. But I say nothing. Can't. I gave up making myself understood a long time ago. Besides, I don't have the vocabulary to describe it. I keep silent, my eyes riveted to the little screen in order to stop seeing or hearing anything. Cling to the images for reasons that have nothing to do with them and without which they would be ineffective.

When the news suddenly shows the traffic circle at the Champs-Elysées, thick with people: a demonstration against somebody named Franco got out of hand in front of the Spanish embassy. People were protesting the execution of a man condemned to death, which was scheduled for dawn; suddenly I feel less alone.

Then it's about the first big drug seizure in France: during a traffic accident on the Champs-Elysées, blocked because of the demonstration, the police unexpectedly discovered several kilos of heroin in the trunk of a car. Arrested, the driver was on his way to avenue Gabriel, it seems. Only I can guess to whose home.

Whatever the case may have been, Fabrice doesn't come to class the next day nor the days that follow. It's explained that the entire Fenwick family has suddenly left France to move to Port-au-Prince or Fort-de-France, I don't remember anymore. At the other end of the world, in any case. That's where they've all disappeared: my best friend, my childhood love, and their mother the goddess. Disappeared without leaving any address, nothing, not the slightest farewell, without my knowing why; then can you suddenly disappear, just like that, heaven and earth vanishing in a second? The party is over. I'm nine years old. Why am I still here? Why am I here? And what's the use, since they took with them my reason for being. Cut me off from myself, abandoned me and left me more like an orphan on this earth than if my parents had been dead. From now on, I no longer have a purpose. I feel as if it's too late. And I'll keep feeling that way.

However, that's when I started to laugh. Isn't everything uproariously absurd? Life impossibly mischievous? You think you're living until what you're really living dies, revives; I had just seen it happen. Everything was only illusion, smoke, movement. Without my knowing it, that fateful day determined the guiding principle of my life: from then on I'd only be aware of appearances and disappearances. Then only am I stimulated, do I rediscover my contours, accede to an age of instinct. My sensations become sensational. Time stirs. I'm alive.

What was I complaining about? Just a little while ago, an apparition knocked on my door and I opened it. I'm blessed. Even my particular case has arrogantly ceased to hold me back. What could it signify in comparison to the truth that had just awakened in me. Since that Sunday in 1969, the vagaries of the self have always seemed pitiful to me. And even more so in others, which has rarely been well taken. It's because very few suspect that phenomena are more astonishing than beings, who are only an avatar of them. It's true that I didn't know anyone who had had the opportunity to live, at the age of nine, an afternoon that summed up, by itself, the material of a hundred years of existence. One day I'd have to pay my debt for having been able to come close to the innermost magic of the world, the rangy absoluteness of life.

And I did pay.

FIFTEEN YEARS LATER, I was in love with a young girl who had dazzled me on the rue de Buci, I was absolutely struck to the quick by her beauty and her dove-gray blouse; yes, dove-gray, I didn't even notice it right then and there, fascinated as I was by its artistic-looking printer's-ink stains, which were like a mysterious Rorschach blot, a speck of the cosmos in negative.

In a second I belonged body and soul to that vision. I clearly felt a click, as if some unknown spirit were suddenly trickling through me. Her name was Fabienne. That very evening, I would take her to Brussels, then to the Channel Islands, where it was freezing. Our story began as a journey.

We lived together for four years.

When I introduced her to my parents, after dinner my mother taunted my father. "You like her, huh!" My father got up to get the dessert in the kitchen. I didn't have any.

As we had our coffee, my mother began praising the girl I'd broken up with a while back, after living together for three years. She missed her. I loved Gaëlle, she was the first girl I'd known, but I was lusting for passion. We were living the contemptible little life of a bohemian couple, which at the time seemed attractive after the rue Marbeuf. But leaving my parents hadn't been enough to make me finally feel free, and Gaëlle suited them too well to be a match for me. Our breakup was slow and painful. Gaëlle had stopped taking drugs since she'd known me, and I was telling myself that I had no right to drop her, although my scruples made her suffer a lot more. One day, I went to see her parents and told them I was planning on leaving their daughter. "I want to see the world," I said. Her mother began weeping. Her father drew nervously on his pipe. I later learned that Gaëlle had spent several months in a psychiatric hospital. I saw her in the street once: she was extremely thin, dressed all in black, and I hid behind a tree to avoid facing what I'd created.

Fabienne was the exact opposite of Gaëlle, just as Laurence would later be the opposite of Fabienne, without reminding me of Gaëlle in any way. Physically, Fabienne was as tall, as beautiful, and as cold as Gaëlle was short, tortured, and sensitive. Moreover, whereas everything had been simple with Gaëlle, Fabienne could only come with a man whom she despised; she loved me; the best I hoped for would backfire on me. We had some appalling nights together. She was endlessly checking to make sure her ass stayed lily white.

After three irreproachable years, she ended up hooking up with a handsome Spaniard who was getting out of prison. Throughout an entire summer she loved despising him. She would deride both of us. When I found out about it, in a rage I threw out the window a little cat we'd found. It struck a pane of glass on the opposite building. Horrified, I looked for it in the darkness. Finally I heard it mewing weakly. A window opened and a woman's voice called it. It was saved.

Fabienne had been sitting on the couch and didn't move a hair. She stayed there like a statue. I slapped her. I regretted it immediately as she rushed into the bathroom to see if I'd left any marks. I didn't know what to do anymore. So I smashed a bottle of ink against the wall, which covered it with spatters, from which surged a monstrous-looking yeti. The stains on her blouse that had fascinated me when we met had just delivered up their secret. By the end of that excruciating night I had exhausted all my jealousy.

The following winter she left me. "Real life is in the United States," she declared. I gave up trying to convince her of her stupidity. I was tired of our story. It hadn't kept any of its promises.

She left. And for the first time I knew what despair was; it seemed horrible, healthy. When you miss one person, everything is repopulated. Every night I put this into painting, drowning in rage and turpentine on canvases twice my size. For entire hours I emptied my guts on dove-colored backgrounds. Revived living harmonies. No matter how cold it got in the room, I never felt it. These were spectacular nights. The spirit of the stains was speaking in me.

Two months later Fabienne called me from my brother's in San Francisco, where I'd sent her. She was at the bottom of a hole. Crying day and night. She wanted me to come get her. She didn't even have enough strength to get back to Paris.

The idea that she was exaggerating didn't enter my mind. It was as if I'd been waiting only for that: leaving. That call from the other end of the world was irresistible.

In fifteen days I'd sold what little I had to pull together the money for the trip and abandoned plans for my first show. I was going to survive on unemployment over there.

Not for an instant did I think I was leaving to get her back. I just had to go there, this was between me and myself, my business. Besides, I was the first to admit that my leaving was ridiculous. My friends thought I was trying to get attention.

At the San Francisco airport, she threw herself into my arms. From that moment on, everything became unreal. We bought a blue metallic Buick Skylark for five hundred dollars and headed east, taking the southern route. It was as if we were outside of time. Driving night and day. Nothing had any meaning. We made love desperately. In every state the police would stop us for speeding, and they even did it by helicopter in the Texas desert. We'd take off immediately to find refuge in another state. Landscapes scrolled by like the tapes by The Cure or Prince that we played in the background. Several times we narrowly missed having an accident. I hadn't even bothered taking out insurance.

Every three or four days we'd stop in a motel to bathe and sleep on clean sheets. We'd park the Buick in a lot, and an electronic machine would deliver the key card to a room where the fuschia carpeting was five inches thick. The plumbing was pure Hollywood. In the morning you slid your Visa card into the machine to get back your car. We'd leave without having seen anyone. It was scary, euphoric.

Then we went over the border. Fabienne wanted to visit the Gulf of Mexico. That is where the death we were looking for awaited us. On a potholed road that led nowhere, a half-dozen Mexican workers chased us to the edge of a pickup-truck trail. Their white headlights surrounded us in the night. We had run into them a bit earlier, and I'd seen in their eyes everything they were dreaming about doing to the blond whose long, tan legs they'd caught sight of in a Buick with a California license plate. Their entire life of humiliation deformed their features with a desire that claimed compensation. There was no hope in being able to talk things over with them. Their spite was terrifying. An hour later they'd made a U-turn and caught up with us.

Trying to shake them was useless. The Buick was bounding over enormous rocks. Knocking into potholes. I couldn't go any faster without risking overturning into a ditch or breaking a wheel. The plain stretched as far as the eye can see, and there was no hope of being saved. Nobody around for miles.

I felt immensely sorry for Fabienne. What was about to happen wouldn't be fun. For me, either. I remember trying to make a joke. Something like: "Come on, it'll all be over in an hour. What's the point of worrying. Life is beautiful." I wasn't being brave, but Fabienne was so terrified as she sat next to me that all my fear went into her, as if it were being absorbed. Tears were flowing down her cheeks, and she had rolled the strap of the camera around her hand. It was the only weapon she'd found. I told her to hide under the dashboard. She huddled up as well as she could and stopped moving.

The Buick was going all over the place, and I was having trouble keeping up speed. Getting to the federal highway in time was impossible. As I drove, I thought, "This is the end of you. Here it is, the end of you, Grégoire. Your journey stops here." Those were the words that came to me. I thought them coldly. They were just an observation. I couldn't think of anything else to tell myself. I was convincing myself that what followed would be nothing but an unpleasant formality that hardly concerned me. But I couldn't get over it: did everything I'd lived have to end up on this crummy road? With this squalid ending? It didn't make any sense. I hadn't experienced anything yet. These men didn't even know us. I figured our bodies would probably never be found. It was even possible that no one would ever find out what happened to us. I studied the landscape. I would have liked to see something, a tree, a bush, a pole, anything at all that would stand up for me. That would at least mark the place. But there was nothing.

Then I became fed up. The farce was difficult enough. I braked and stopped the Buick in the middle of the road. Let's get it over with. I was ready. The pickup stopped as well. Its white headlights blazed less than thirty feet behind us. I switched off the ignition. Then there was total silence. Through the windshield you could see the wind sweeping the plain. It was a magnificent night. Phosphorescent. Thousands of stars. The glove compartment wasn't completely shut. I saw my hands on the wheel. Nothing happened. They weren't coming. Fabienne had straightened up and, like me, was waiting. But what the hell were they doing?! I swore out loud and took off violently again with the Buick. Immediately the pickup shot forward. It caught up to us in a second; I thought it was going to ram against us, but against all expectation the men passed us and took off into the night. We looked at each other. At every moment I was expecting to find the pickup parked sideways across the road. But no. It had disappeared and didn't materialize again. Three hours later we drove across the U.S. border.

The customs officer to whom we told the story of our unpleasant experience nodded his head. "Everyone in the region is armed," he said. "When you stopped the car, they must have thought you were ready to take them on and they didn't have the nerve to attack you. They must have told themselves that there'd be deaths. You were very lucky."

That night was destined to be ours: as we drove north, we went through a forest. Hundreds of deer were grazing at the side of the road. Maybe thousands. And others were still coming out of the undergrowth. Gently I drove the Buick onto the grass. The deer barely moved aside. They gamboled in the harsh light of the headlights. It must have been their usual time. The young ones were rolling in the clover. I cut the motor. On the warm hood of the Buick, Fabienne came in my arms for the first time. She was the first to be surprised by it. She hadn't thought it possible. Her face was all red and she began to laugh like a child. Suddenly she felt light. So, she did have the capacity to be happy without despising. The curse had been lifted. But she'd had to rub shoulders with death to achieve it. This was an important night for her. Shortly afterward, we went back to France.

In the plane, I felt incredibly serene. It had nothing to do with Fabienne. It was as if I had gotten back in touch with my story. Accomplished what I had to. For once, things hadn't been aborted. This wasn't like the golf game that had been canceled. The thought came to me in a completely incongruous fashion. It loomed up out of oblivion, and it was like an illumination. All by itself, and for the past four years, the word *golf* had seemed to sum up my life; yes, everything fit into this little four-letter word that had taken control of my imagination ever since Madame Fenwick had held out the prospect of it to me fifteen years earlier, as the culmination of a bliss that, in the end, I'd been denied. Without my suspecting it, it had become my emblem of happiness, just as staphylococcus aureus had played that role for death.

I remembered that when I'd met Fabienne, I'd wanted to take her "outside Paris," the only indication that I'd had regarding the location of that golf game Madame Fenwick had promised me. Yet again, my desire had revealed its intentions from the start: in her dove-gray blouse, Fabienne was the one who had to satisfy the memory that remained unfulfilled. And in fact, she succeeded in leading me into that vast golf game that ultimately was our improvident journey across the United States, to that second-to-last hole of golf—or should I say "Gulf" . . . of Mexico—into which both of us nearly fell; but in the end, everything ended happily on the *green*, among the deer. Now I understood the impulse that had pushed me to leave everything to go to the other side of the ocean. It was where my golf had to be invented, farther away from Paris than I'd imagined, as if the dimensions of the myth had to be measured at the greatest geographical distance. As I got off the plane, I loved life dearly.

Back in Paris, we were out of money. Had no place to sleep. Fabienne's sister, Laurence, put us up. But the situation couldn't go on forever. One afternoon, when we were having a drink at the Café de Flore, a journalist we vaguely knew walked through the room. I pressured Fabienne to go and see him. She had a press card, and maybe he'd have work for her. She didn't have the nerve. I made fun of her. She went up to him. They sat at another table. An hour later they left together. Through the windows of the café I saw that he was putting his arm around her. One year later, I learned by chance in a newspaper about the birth of their first daughter.

That was how she walked out of my life, by walking out of that café without a word and without turning around, after all we'd experienced, not even a look, nothing, never to appear again nor offer any news for ten years. What a disappearing act! I came close to being locked up. By the following day, my hair had turned white on one side. I never got over it. Then what kind of nose did I have, me, who lacked a sense of smell, for sniffing out from the crowd the one person capable of reproducing Madame Fenwick's disappearance, even though it had seemed so unsurpassable fifteen years before? History repeats itself as caricature, I snickered out loud in the streets. Before telling myself that maybe history itself is produced by repetition.

I didn't know where to go, and for three whole months I lived in the street, surviving on what was left of my unemployment, wandering through the day without any longer knowing who I was, sleeping till dawn in stairwells. I no longer knew anyone, and no one knew me anymore. Yet I wasn't alone. The entire time I was hearing voices, which ordered me to turn left or right, or walk straight ahead, or whinny, because in one night a horse had grown inside me (it's huge, the body of a horse).

The voices weren't evil; but if they'd ordered me to kill people I didn't know or throw myself into the unknown, I would have obeyed them just the same. These fits could last for two or three hours, usually casting their spell on me late morning, around eleven-thirty. All that was necessary was the angle of a straw in a glass, a word overheard in a conversation, the coded language of a stoplight at a corner for them to carry me through the city. Everything was a sign.

The voices arrived unexpectedly and disappeared in the same way, leaving me dumbfounded and at the same time filled with a feeling of power that nothing could change, be it cold or hunger. I was the nameless master of time. The elect of the netherworld. The incarnation of universal spontaneity.

I didn't know what their intention was, but when the voices ceased, I would invariably come to in front of a commemorative plaque attached to the pediment of a building. However, my name was never engraved on it. Or else, I was all the great people who'd disappeared. In this way, my wanderings became marble. The entire city had become a cemetery, throughout which I walked surrounded by countless deaths, like a ghost in search of a grave. For once, life and death were reconciled.

When the voices left me alone, another kind of frenzy would take hold of me: writing everything that happened to me in the margins of whatever newspaper I got hold of, a medium that quickly seemed the most propitious in my situation. Because in the midst of the others in this demeaning world, I was trying to send out news of myself, in order to reassure the whole earth about my fate and not disappear altogether. Humanity was also depending on me, and still is today, as it does on each of us.

I remember a sentence that I tirelessly scrawled on everything I came across, like a talisman I would put up everywhere: "The way was lost along the road; well, then there is a road." I didn't know which, but that certitude kept me on my feet. What I was living wasn't as miserable and incoherent as it seemed. There was a reason for my decline. It might have even been an opportunity. I didn't lose confidence; despite everything, the future existed.

As a matter of fact, when the whole thing was over, I realized that for three whole months I'd been nine years old in the body of a man of thirty in order to remove a proscription I'd been left with at that age. And if a demonstration had once again stood in my way, this time it was madness, the ultimate protest of life when death is arbitrarily imposed upon it. Everything was being transposed, deepening in variations. The same scenes were happening again, my story was unfolding accordingly, but under another angle, the cosine of the former.

Thus, it wasn't a member of the riot squad who sent me back home; one day when it was too cloudy, I went to sit in a public garden and began talking out loud to an imaginary little girl, who listened to me for a long time, quietly sitting next to me on a bench. It was Marie-Blanche, who'd returned to me in spirit. From the end of the world, she was suddenly appearing to give me courage. And with her the tears that I'd been holding back for more than twenty years.

She hadn't changed. Her lovely, open face, her thoughtful look, the minuscule scar on her chin, her square-cut black hair illuminating her skin, olive as it was: time had changed none of it. And she, as well, recognized me. My love hadn't forgotten me. We were finally reunited. I got well immediately. And from that moment, the voices stopped, no longer appearing except in the form of amorphous anxieties that, sporadically, on some nights, left me petrified with terror at the edge of a precipice that insidiously stirred some part of me while murmuring my name.

Shortly after, I remembered that I had parents and rang at their door. Twenty years later, then, the same circumstances were bringing me back to them. At that moment, I didn't pay attention to it because oblivion was directing my steps to such an extent. I didn't know for three months that this had only brought me back to the scene of that fateful Sunday when everything had changed radically for me. In an infallible way, and without knowing it, I was passing through the same hours, which in time had become weeks. The minutes, as well, were expanding, and blooming.

THIS IS WHY I STAYED at my parents for a time proportional to the one that I'd needed twenty years earlier to have dinner in front of the television, before I went to bed and forgot everything. They asked no questions, nor did they embarrass me in any way, taking me in as simply as possible. This time, far from infuriating me, their discretion made me feel obliged to them.

But they still couldn't do anything for me. Nor could the television, which I wasn't thinking of watching in hopes of discovering an explanation for what had happened to me, as I had at the age of nine. I'd found something better, which was, in fact, the very miracle I needed: Homer's *Odyssey*, which I read in a single transfigured night.

Never before had I known a similar experience with a book, and I never have since. It was as if I was offering my face to the sun. Every verse seemed to be written for me and infused itself in me, flowing through my eyes and my ears. I was the reading itself.

Or rather, it was *The Odyssey* that was figuring me out. Because suddenly everything was clarified by its light. Incredible coincidences arose between what I was reading and what I was living, boundaries were abolished and I could see between the lines where I myself had gone. Implicit in Ulysses' adventures was the revelation of mine, which weren't identical, but resumptions. Charybdis and Scylla, the Cattle of the Sun, the Cyclops . . . in my own way I'd lived all that. I could cite places and dates. Pick up the thread. Weren't the voices that I'd been hearing those of the dead who preoccupy Ulysses once he is in hell? The souls of heroes had sought to recount their stories to me, as well. Does that mean that I'd descended into hell? Then *The Odyssey* was the oracle who informed me of my future . . . I sometimes had to put down the book to get my breath back.

I thought about my lovers next. I'd known four worthy of that name, as had Ulysses in all of *The Odyssey*. Everything checked out. For me, Calypso, Circe, Nausicaa, and Penelope had faces. I knew their old addresses. Still had photos. The nymph was the one I'd photographed nude in a bathtub during a vacation in Corsica (like Ulysses, I was tired of her and dreaming of leaving); the magician had posed for me illuminated by sunlight in the Texas desert (her bold beauty didn't change me into a swine, but into a horse); the daughter of the king had left me a snapshot of her fondling herself in front of me (like all young girls, every day she would go to wash her family's dirty laundry in the river, and I was the river); as for Penelope, a class photo showed her in the first row, surrounded by all the suitors. It was like Odysseus's four. North, south, east, and west. Winter, fall, spring, summer. Judith, Rachel . . . As for Athena, protectoress of the hero with a thousand expedients, need I mention her again?

I also remembered that little engraving that circulated illicitly at the end of Louis XIV's reign. It showed the Sun King surrounded by four women he had loved, and each of them was placing a hand somewhere on his body: Mlle de la Vallière on his heart, Mme de Fontanges on his scrotum, Mme de Montespan on his sex, and Mme de Maintenon on his crown. He, as well, was a new Ulysses.

When I had finished reading, morning was coming without my being aware of it. My parents had left for work. I was alone in my childhood room. But everything had changed. For the first time in a long time I was calm. *The Odyssey* was lying the foot of my bed. I hadn't marked a single line. It was useless. Hadn't it finally found the road where my way had been lost? For an entire night my hands had held the map of time, and from now on I could locate my wanderings on it and get my bearings in the world. I didn't know what compass guided others in life, and whether they really found their way by means of money or something else that was cold and impersonal, but it no longer concerned me.

It didn't matter whether I was wrong or right; that wasn't the question. I was right. There was a mythological dimension to beings and situations, and it gave reality a range that it is usually refused. Although my existence no longer made any sense, *The Odyssey* was giving a positive Homeric meaning to everything I was experiencing. The book was teaching me about life from a new angle. It was affixing antique seals to my distress. And they're still there.

Why would I have allowed myself to be convinced that I should get help if it was to suffer a despair that wouldn't be used for anything but demeaning myself or others? If it meant really getting ill or wasting energy under the aegis of programmed compensations, which would lead to more specific and more complete unhappiness. I've never tried to be as reasonable. If I was nothing in the eyes of the world or any individual, I existed for *The Odyssey*, and that finally legitimized my presence on earth. The book had baptized me. I wasn't Ulysses, such a mix-up had never crossed my mind, but the cycle was perpetuated through me. I could call myself happy.

You can think of it what you will, but believing myself to be a new Ulysses was worth more than taking myself for a modern man. If I compared one fiction to another, mine was bringing me freedom of movement. It was giving me the power to say no to the ludicrous laws of this world. My mind wasn't social anymore. Neither was my body. Without needing to deny these things, I was eluding common imperatives as if by magic.

Human resources are infinite: I was on the street but hadn't I found, without even planning it, a refuge of more than ten thousand verses, much more spacious than forty-three hundred square feet on avenue Gabriel? No one could ever evict me from *The Odyssey*. For once, it was a temple reserved for the riches of the mind. A church without a priest for a religion revealed to me alone. Moreover, I'd never needed to take legal or illegal drugs (aside from tobacco). My antiquity is a more hallucinogenic substance—it's always a matter of inventing your own god, a form of sublimation for yourself alone. Should someone else think of making *The Odyssey* his god, I'd have to change religions. Even at the worst moments, my life has never disappointed me. I had found my formula.

Therefore, I've sometimes ended up frequenting people only because they represented a character in *The Odyssey,* without their suspecting it (I'm not that crazy). It has brought me relationships vaster and more unforeseen than those based on advantage or fear, as is the rule everywhere. I didn't hope for much more from my contemporaries.

The days that followed that Homeric night were longer than usual. Still, I had to do something. I didn't know what. In which direction to go? I went back to the café in which the woman who had so superbly incarnated the ghost of Madame Fenwick had disappeared three months earlier. I stayed there. For entire hours I waited for someone to come say goodbye to me, anyone at all, just a goodbye, to keep me from wandering in an eternity that was dead and gone; but people would say hello and I'd remain seated, incapable of getting up and leaving, endlessly brooding and observing the stupefied world from the same table while drinking the same coffee every day.

I was spending my time reading and writing in notebooks. In my situation it was no longer a question of painting, if not with words. Also, painting was part of a former life. Not for anything in the world would I have made the journey back to reclaim that Eurydice. I never touched a brush again. It was my sacrifice for continuing to live, just as my father had put away his drum set.

One afternoon, a very young girl came to sit at my table. Without my asking her anything, she offered me the studio she was moving out of on rue Saint-Lazare, with three months paid in advance. I'm sticking to recounting the thing just as it happened. The name of the street seemed terribly propitious to me.

Two days later, she was handing over the keys to me. Everything had happened as if by magic. Standing on the sidewalk, I didn't know how to thank her. She was happy just to smile and say goodbye, and she disappeared down the street. She was in a hurry because she had to pick up her laundry at the dry cleaner's before it closed. At the time I hardly paid any attention to this detail; but thinking of it that evening, I burst out laughing inside: didn't I owe my opportunity to a pure manifestation of Nausicaa, who, according to *The Odyssey*, meets Ulysses while on the way to the river to wash her clothes? That's how I lived my life at the time.

AND IT CONTINUED. Because shortly after, I found work in the most unexpected way: after a chess game in a bar, my opponent told me that the telex office of the press agency where he was working was looking for someone to write dispatches. When I went there, the head of the agency asked me for a résumé; I explained that more than ten thousand verses by Homer had been needed to give an account of Ulysses' life. It made him smile. He hired me. My likable kookiness could come in handy, he must have thought. Consequently, fifteen days were enough for me to get back on my feet, as they say. I had work and a place to live. I could breathe a little. Nothing is ever permanent.

If *The Odyssey* was telling the truth, I must have gone to Alcinous, the father of Nausicaa. The one who is said to have brought Ulysses, the awakened hero par excellence, to his home to sleep. I wondered what it could mean. Was I supposed to doze off at the office? I tried it one afternoon; an hour later a coworker was shaking me roughly: I hadn't traveled a millimeter. Apparently it wasn't a question of this kind of sleep. Which, then?

What is more, nothing happened as foreseen. Alcinous wasn't at all like a king; at the agency, everybody called him Auntie, and once or twice a week, he'd come press against me from behind while I was typing out dispatches on the keyboard. He'd stay unmoving behind my back for a long time, without saying anything, brushing against me, I could feel his breath on my back, and I had the smarmy impression that he was breathing in my odor, immersing himself in it on the sly, while his breathing quickened, like sighs that reminded me of my brother when I'd joined him in his bed; I was frozen with hate.

Sometimes I'd turn around suddenly. I was ready to start a fight. But each time Auntie smiled at me with a soft, innocent expression, his face had a deathly sick sweetness that was impossible to interpret, and I'd start to doubt his attitude. I knew, nevertheless, that I wasn't inventing anything. But it was impossible to unmask him. Without saying anything I'd go back to work. A block of granite in my stomach. Auntie would linger a little while longer behind me. Then he'd leave and shut himself up in his office, from which he'd emerge a half-hour later with red and tortured eyes. I'd feel demolished.

This situation would last for several months. I put up with it stoically. I didn't want to go back to the street. This time, it wouldn't have had any appeal. So I'd make myself inconspicuous. I let the others debate the great problems of the hour in the cafeteria, as if they had a grip on them. To listen to them, social organization was threatened everywhere, and it was urgent to defend it. I'd stare at my plate. Some of them would question me in a friendly tone: didn't I agree that this society was horrible and that we had to mobilize to make it better; and I'd answer that bettering what was appalling was making it worse yet. Those who had no experience were the most relentless about criticizing my offhand manner. I didn't even try to explain to them that my ambition wasn't to exist in this world, but to make a world exist.

As for Auntie, he never shut up about the fate of those who were suffering just about everywhere on the planet; but to hear him, you'd think that none of us were living on this earth. He was an activist in various NGOs. People admired his engagement. In his office he'd tacked up a brochure showing a Palestinian adolescent wearing no shirt, sitting on a big rock, and holding a gun between his thighs, from which protruded a yellow flower. He would look longingly at it when he had someone in his office. His pants hung off him, he had an extremely flat ass and wouldn't allow anyone to pass behind him. Sometimes he called me Grégorius, like my brother when he couldn't prevent himself from expressing in a dead language his desire that something be added to the back-end of words.

It was in this fraternal environment that I earned my living. For eighty-five hundred francs a month, my job was to compose, in fewer than sixty characters, news items about children killing each other as they got out of school, husbands cutting their wives' throats, mothers smothering their babies, not to mention suicides and new Ulysses who were beginning, logically enough when all is said and done, to bump off with heavy weapons all the suitors that they ran into on the street. As somebody who was dreaming of ten thousand verses, it was quite a punishment to write news bytes of two lines.

To avoid becoming mad from powerlessness, I began to invent dispatches and secretly distribute them. Sabotage is the only weapon that remains within reach of everyone.

One evening, I sent out to all subscribers the sad news that Auntie had died; his car crashed into a tree in a small birch forest. As soon as I wrote "small birch forest," my last name started to shake with pleasure. Trembling all over, I sent the news. It was a perfect crime: no one would be able to find the body of the person who in one second became more dead to me than if I'd strangled him with my own hands. From that day on, I learned to live with myself. Nobody realized my joke. That was even more enlightening. The enterprise that had been tying my body in knots had just bit the dust. I wasn't dead yet.

A few weeks later, the Berlin Wall came down. The telex machines made us live, minute by minute, this magnificent event that was going to change our lives and reconcile humanity with itself; we were living, it seems, the "end of history."

One afternoon, I got up suddenly from my workstation. I'd had enough. What had my life become? I had some friends in Berlin. They lived in the Kreuzberg district, the only place in Europe where existence seemed to have a certain appeal. The fall of the wall spelled the end of the life they were leading there, and they had to be the only people who weren't sharing in the general euphoria. They were the ones I wanted to be around. I walked out on my job. That same evening, I was strolling down Orianen Strasse. It was while coming back from Berlin by train that I would meet the woman who'd revive my staphylococcus aureus. While the entire world was reveling in the "end of history," I chose that moment to pick up the thread of mine. In a way, Alcinous really had taken me home. But why would I say again what I've already said.

IT'S OFTEN FORGOTTEN that at the end of *The Odyssey*, Ulysses leaves Penelope to go off again, by road this time. He's finished with the sea and turns his back to it. But he has to take a long oar with him. One day, reveals the oracle, someone will ask him what he is doing with a baker's shovel on his shoulder. Then Ulysses will know that he must plant his oar in the earth and found a kingdom. If I do hope for something more, it's only for a pun that will designate with another term what I drag along with me all the time — just as the Evangelists in their time called a cross what their hero, who'd arrived at the end of his odyssey, was carrying on his back.

That said, my paternal grandfather had had less luck than Ulysses: when he got back to his home in 1945 after four years of captivity in a stalag, it was to find out that he'd been accused of bigamy and that his wife was asking for a divorce. An investigation revealed that a soldier from the Wehrmacht had used his papers for a fake identity to marry a Frenchwoman, who'd been abandoned at the time of the collapse of the Nazis.

If that bad joke deprived my grandfather of the joys of his homecoming, my grandmother, who was under the impression that her husband was a bastard, had to squelch her anger. For years on end, she locked herself in the bathroom and spent hours piercing the skin on her face with a pair of scissors.

When she wasn't disfiguring herself, my grandmother, who'd studied art when she was young, would sculpt perfect cherub faces out of cotton.

Her work was impressive enough for Galeries Lafayette to entrust her with the decoration of their windows for Christmas. Everything was ready, my grandmother had managed to transform miles of cotton into a manger with all the figures, when they found out that nothing was fireproof. Despite all the effort, the project was canceled.

My grandmother packed her work in cardboard boxes. But one night, she woke up and in a half-sleep scrawled a few words on a sheet of paper; in the morning, she found on the paper a list of products, which she ran to the city to buy. Returning, she shut herself up in the bathroom; when she came out of it, she had found the way to fireproof cotton.

My grandmother never explained this feat, nor revealed to anyone the secret of her discovery. However, manufacturers came from all over France; Japanese emissaries even found their way to Saint-Germain-en-Laye to offer her a fortune. She stuck to her guns.

That Christmas, my grandmother's flameless cotton-wadding works were the admiration of those passing through boulevard Haussmann. And the next Christmas too, because they were such a success.

As for my grandfather, he devoted his evenings to archiving tons of files that he never finished putting in order on the living room table. When there was a soccer game on television, he would get up at the first goal that signaled "We're done for" and grumblingly turn off the set. He no longer thought that you could reverse missing the boat.

He called his wife "Pussy" and never by her first name. One time, he put a hand on my shoulder and said to me in a serious tone, "The important thing with women is to make them laugh."

His father lived with them. We called him "the other grandfather." He cursed God and zealots. To annoy his daughter-in-law, he waited for her to get up and prepare breakfast every morning; then he'd leap out of his room naked as a jaybird and at the age of seventy do his exercises in front of her.

Aunt Jotte was my grandmother's eldest sister. One morning, she woke up with a black spot on her cheek. The next day, the spot was a small mark; every day it got larger, devouring her face. She died in a few weeks from a metastasized cancer. Her face, which had turned completely black, stuck with me for a long time. When Uncle Jacky arrived at his wife's funeral, he was driving the superb-looking white Citroën DS that for years he'd been so proud of. I alone seemed to make the connection with the black goddess that Aunt Jotte had ended up becoming, because DS in French sounds just like *déesse,* which means "goddess."

ON THE EXACT DAY of my eighteenth birthday, I left my parents' home. I wasn't a minor anymore. I thought my life was going to begin all over again.

But one fine afternoon, my mother calls. Her voice is weird and thick-sounding and founders and veers out of control. She tells me she loves me, loves me so much, if I only knew . . . I think she's drunk, but not only. She admits to me that she's just taken some pills. "So what!" she says, her voice getting louder. "The important thing is that I love you, if you only knew how I love you, I wanted to tell you before . . ."

It isn't the first time that my mother has attempted suicide. The last three Christmas Eves have already been the occasion to wish the medics a happy one at the emergency room. And several times she has explained away her suddenly bandaged wrists by her clumsiness in handling the big bread knife. My brother and I avoid finding out any more about it.

But that day I can't avoid anything. I squeeze the receiver in my hand while my mother's voice at the other end of the line grows fainter. I imagine that she's squirming next to the telephone because aside from getting weaker, her voice is whimpering, and sometimes sounds distant. I try to make her talk as much as possible so that she doesn't fall asleep; at the same time I need to hang up to call for help while she's still alive. I keep walking in circles in my bedroom. But the telephone cord gets tangled, so I begin turning in the other direction.

I finally hang up and immediately notify my father at work. Then I dash into the subway. This is the day that three controllers choose to question me for not having a ticket. I shout at them to let me by, my mother has just tried to commit suicide. They snicker with a knowing look. To the inspector who writes up my offense on a pink stub I blurt, "That's all the literature you're capable of." Her jaw tenses and the pen between her fingers begins to tremble. Around me her two colleagues get threatening. I don't insist. On the platform is a pub-

licity poster that I read as I DID THE RIGHT THING BY
VOMITING. It really says I DID THE RIGHT THING BY
VACUUMING.

When I get to rue Marbeuf, the medics are already
there. But this must be another day because, in my
memory, I am now twelve and returning from school.
The house is swarming with emergency medics, and I
don't understand why. My mother, in her nightgown, is
lying on the couch in the living room. She's deathly pale,
and her expression shatters space with its bitterness. In
a corner of the living room, two medics are putting away
the tube and other materials that I'll have other occa-
sions to learn are used to pump stomachs.

I sit down next to the window, where I'll be out of the
way. My father is filling out papers with the fire chief.
The latter says that he has to take my mother to the
hospital; but she absolutely refuses to go; huddled, she
looks like a ferocious animal. She keeps repeating into
space that they should have let her die. She's always so
dolled up, but now her hair is a sight to behold.

After several attempts to reason with her or speak
sternly to her as if to a child, the chief resigns himself
to giving up, provided that my mother will agree to get

help from a psychiatrist. My mother condescends with a scornful gesture and turns her head toward the wall.

Then everyone begins to wait in the living room. There's a long silence that leads to nothing. My father asks me if I had a good day in school. My mother's still on the couch alone, her expression adamant. You can see through to her little breasts, sagging like the rest of her body. The psychiatrist finally arrives, and the medics leave immediately, their boots in the stairway making the entire building shake.

As soon as she sees the psychiatrist, my mother acerbically makes fun of the camelhair coat that he is taking off and putting next to me. He squats down to my mother's level and tries to start a conversation with her. For every response, my mother spreads her thighs and bursts out laughing in his face. Despite myself, I catch sight of her vagina. It's as dark as her hair is blond, and that perplexes me. Another mystery. One more. But now isn't the moment to resolve it, and I content myself with observing the psychiatrist's strategies for getting my mother to open up.

Standing back, my father listens, chews his lower lip, his elbow resting on the cornice of the mantelpiece.

Sometimes he intercedes with a thin voice to add a detail, smooth out the sharp edges, minimize the drama. My mother grumbles and fidgets every time, full of contempt and arrogance. She talks about her disgust for life. The pointlessness of it all. In any case, she'll try again. Several times she repeats in a hard voice, "But what a lousy life!" Her nightgown is draped over her pallid legs, which are covered with black-and-blue marks.

When the session is over, the psychiatrist rises and takes my father aside. He talks to him about psychiatric follow-up, treatments. Says that there's nothing he can do right now. My mother has to come to his office. He's already holding his card in one hand. My father is worried about the charges. On the couch, my mother shuts her eyes, suddenly looking so old, so tiny. So alone.

The psychiatrist makes out a prescription, which he hands to my father. Then his eyes seek his camelhair coat. Which causes them to fall upon me. He stares at me, and, for the first time in my life, I have the impression that someone is really seeing me. His look is saying that I exist. I've stopped being transparent. All of a sudden, I have a body. A soul. He has seen me. He saw. He has understood. He knows. He's going to tell them. He's going to tell them that there've been enough horrors. Maybe he's even going to take me with him in a little while, until things have improved at home, and I can stop being a washcloth that was put in a corner.

I keep staring at the psychiatrist. He starts to move toward my father. I sense that he's going to speak, I'm sure of it, he's looking for the words, he doesn't want to wound anyone, I understand; but I see him slipping into his camelhair coat and taking the check that my father had filled out on the mantelpiece as he suppressed a grimace. He doesn't say a word. Doesn't even try to. Shortly after, he leaves without looking at me, and with him something infinite in me.

Sitting on my chair, I suddenly have the very clear perception that this time it's not simply a matter of a bad moment to get through. Events don't end by themselves as I thought they did but prolong themselves through their consequences, which in turn become events, and so on. The innocence of the future is a pile of shit, I realize in a flash. It's too late. The life waiting for me is already loaded with catastrophes that are doing it in from the beginning. I've been folded into a dark, permanent habit, as if into a pleat, which has shut me up in darkness and is even claiming the right to become a part of me. Yes, something has been disrupted, I don't know what, but I have the hunch that I haven't finished hearing about it. So I tell myself that I'm in big trouble.

I'm going to have to dig in. Harden myself deep down, under a smiling exterior, so that they'll leave me alone.

For a long time, in my bed, I've been telling myself the story of the psychiatrist going home that evening; he's sitting on the edge of the bed and telling his wife about the visit he just made to us. He's saying that he would have liked to do something for the kid. But it was impossible. His wife understands that it was. She, as well, thinks it's too bad for the kid. She's touched at sensing how sad and demoralized her husband is, and she puts her arms around him. She's proud of his compassion. Then they talk about something else, and I cease to exist for them.

I don't know how many times I fell asleep imagining that scene, like a dream I created before having none as I slept. But when I wake up, I spit on that rotten psychiatrist who caused a terrible hope to be born in me and abandoned me with this hideous consciousness concerning my fate that I currently have, because of him.

Afterward, paying attention to what nobody cares about became second nature to me. It was enough for someone to look in one direction for me to make him feel ashamed not to be looking in another, at something better, which he was refusing to see. I was spending my time harassing every glance I came across. The blindness was global, and I was waging a merciless struggle to make the world finally open its eyes to what was worth the trouble, rather than this put-on that it criminally insisted on continuing to contemplate. Politically, I became intractable: everything that was perceived as negligible was bound to be concealing the greatest quality. In the end, it developed into a habit. It didn't always make me clever; what in the eyes of others has no importance sometimes really has none; nor was it constantly me being forgotten in a corner that I had to salvage at any price. No, the world wasn't a psychiatrist cravenly averting his eyes at every moment. As a matter of fact, seeing the state we all were in, it was worse.

AGE THIRTEEN. Every morning I pry up a pebble below our place and kick it all the way to rue Clerc, in the neighborhood known as Gros Caillou, meaning "Big Pebble," where my junior high school is. Despite all the traps waiting for us, I get it there safe and sound, happy about allowing it to travel. In this way I feel as if I'm modifying something immutable in the universe. Once a car came close to running me over while I went to the middle of place de l'Alma to get the pebble back. Invariably, we separate at the corner of rue Clerc, where I kick it into the mouth of a sewer. Each time, I wish it good luck. I imagine the fantastic voyages it will have, whereas I have to stay here. At least it will have some adventures. And that's thanks to me. It's my representative in other places. Maybe it will turn up again. Sometimes, before making it disappear into the mouth of a sewer, I kiss it passionately. This ritual goes on for an entire school year.

That was the year that Béatrice appeared. Coeducation had just been introduced in French schools, and she was the only girl to come to our class. Our bitter disappointment would barely last: she was white water, and seeing her could make you believe in fields of mimosa in the middle of Paris. She wasn't shy. Her breasts were rolling in gold.

In a few days, the whole class was eating out of her hand. All she needed was to make a gesture, and ten faces turned quickly in her direction. It was about who'd carry her bag, do her homework, give her trinkets. Béatrice would laugh. Offer favors without ever granting them. Create rivalries. Her many suitors would protect her. I refused to be a part of it. It was a farce that infuriated me. I'd snicker to see my friends grovel to please her. In her presence they were reduced to slush; but they made vulgar jokes as soon as they were alone together.

I didn't want to sit up and beg. Not even entertain the idea. I still preferred being unpleasant. One day when she asked me to carry her bag, I retorted that she certainly did have her share of lackeys. What was so great about her dazzling smiles if they were the reward for being reduced to her poodle? Although I wasn't claiming to be any better than the others, I had no intention of being a part of it.

Of all the suitors, however, I was the one chosen by Béatrice! At the end of the school year, she took my hand as we got out of class and led me into a small park. The June sun illuminated her. She was the first girl in my life I kissed. Her tongue curled around mine. At first I was taken aback: then I found everything fantastic. It took place underneath a big chestnut tree, which hasn't dared move since. At the end of the week, Béatrice left for vacation. I thought about her all summer.

The following fall I got to the first day of school very early. I was in a hurry to find her. But she had changed districts. I wasn't that surprised. I'd been familiar with disappearances for a long time. The opposite would even have astonished me.

I went to class. The first was chemistry. We had to do an exercise. I solved it in less than two tries, suddenly discovering that I knew the rule of three. I knew the rule of three despite the fact that the calculation had tortured me the entire preceding year, ruined my morale to the point of panic, put up a wall. Two months earlier, I'd been incapable of doing a rule of three, and suddenly, without the slightest effort nor even thinking about it, I knew the rule of three without its being explained to me; beginning with the first class in chemistry, I knew how to postulate and solve a rule of three, I understood what it was as if I'd always known, as well as that the rule of three was something obvious that had been part of me since birth.

For entire months I postulated rules of three everywhere: on tables, my bed, my parents' faces, the streets, even the ceiling. Everything was nothing but a rule of three, which I would solve frenziedly, at every moment. The world was an easy rule of three.

Such euphoria would last through the entire first semester, during which I wondered what secret unified the rule of three, Béatrice and our kiss. What was the nature of that accidental encounter? If my first flirtation had revealed the rule of three to me, what kind of discovery could I expect when I'd make love? And what if it were with two women? Three in the same bed, like my parents? Conversely, what to make of the discovery of the law of Avogadro-Ampère? The commodification of the world? Suddenly everything seemed connected, participating in an essential totality that recomposed over and over, despite barriers, separations, and appearances; I would have had to work like a dog for a long time to understand the rule of three if its secret hadn't been part of this.

From that day on, I knew that you never come face to face with anything, because everything is smoke and mirrors, the condensation of something else, a problem of algebra or the heart. Béatrice hadn't disappeared in vain: she was still there, having become an algebraic sprite, with me wherever I went; you don't separate continents and get away with it.

A young woman to whom I told this story confided in me that she had been a dud when it came to spelling and punctuation in school. Until she had her first period; suddenly, she stopped making mistakes and developed an ease in writing that she thought she'd been denied. The rules of grammar, which up to then had seemed abominable, suddenly ceased to be a mystery for her, as if by magic.

Then I remembered that it was that summer that I'd awakened one night with pins and needles in my entire body. My skin was crawling and I couldn't stop twisting and turning on my bed, as if it were burning. Nothing hurt, but I wanted to scream. I ground my teeth, but it was as if a force were tearing me apart, and I moaned while smothering my voice in my bolster. I felt miserable. I couldn't keep myself from rubbing my chest, my skin, everywhere; I was full of prickles; at the foot of my bed my toes were wriggling in every direction. It was delightful and horrifying at the same time. What was happening to me? My eyes began to well with exasperated tears. I couldn't stand this tension that was wringing out my blood. But it was stronger than me. I kissed the bolster with open mouth and drooled on it. I wanted to rip it apart or do something that could finally calm me down. I felt as if I were embracing a living body, and I buried myself completely in the feathers. I felt robbed of myself. Fallen. I was about to burst into sobs. When I heard myself calling Béatrice. Yes, it was she, Béatrice, her face, lips, I couldn't stop moaning her name, I was ashamed, but I was calling her while I hugged my bolster, wallowed in it, suddenly rearing up to ride it furiously and lay into it with my loins, as if impelled by some mysterious force.

When I noticed that the bolster under me was wet. I pulled away sharply; it was covered with stains, like snot woven with sticky strands. Frantically I wiped myself on my covers. It had a strange salty taste that lasted at the bottom of your throat. I turned the bolster onto its dry side. I listened to my brother's breathing above me; he seemed not to have noticed anything. I huddled against the wall. I didn't want to think about anything anymore. It wasn't true that I'd kissed my bolster, and all the rest. That wasn't me. I would have known if such a thing were normal. I would have been told.

At the same time, I had the beneficent feeling that a weight had just been lifted from me.

After that night, I begin to lead an umpteenth double life. Mornings and evenings I masturbated in secret under my covers while thinking of Béatrice. At the end of summer, I proudly count the hairs beginning to grow on me. I pull on them to speed up the process. On the day when one of the hairs stays between my fingers, I stop. All that day I was devastated.

This is the period when I discover American comics, eagerly following the adventures of those heroes who have to hide their superpowers from the world, which isolates them. Didn't I myself have superpowers that came to me one night in the same way that Doctor Banner suddenly changed into the Incredible Hulk?

IT WAS IN THE EIGHTIES, I don't remember the exact date, but it doesn't matter. Pina Bausch's Tanztheater de Wuppertal was giving a dance performance at the Théâtre de la Ville. A master swimmer in red bathing trunks, strutting around like a rooster, appeared to announce intermission. Like everyone else, I got up to stretch my legs and walked past the rows. When I noticed a female dancer who'd stayed onstage. Standing in the half-light of the scenery, she remained unmoving, her head lowered. Her bearing was unbelievably pathetic.

Immediately I was sure that something abnormal was happening. Despite the distance, I felt a tension emanating from her, something unspeakable that kept her frozen in place and petrified the air. No one seemed to notice anything, and the fact that I did terrified me. Could it be

139

that no one made a distinction between what's contrived and what isn't? This wasn't a manufactured emotion, of that I was certain. The audience passed in front of the stage, some of them intrigued, but not to the point of stopping and going back from where they'd come, impelled as they were by the unalterable need to go smoke a cigarette, take a piss, or have a drink, while talking about everything and nothing with the same imperviousness to the drama that was taking place right next to them.

She could have died at any moment, it was even obvious, her life was hanging by a thread, so couldn't anybody see that death was at her heels, ready to carry her away? Why did I have to be the only one to realize it? I wanted to tear apart those people like sheets of paper. At the same time, I was reasoning with myself. The dancer onstage during intermission was part of the performance, it was supposed to provoke the audience, it was a way of signifying that the show was continuing even when it had stopped—unless it was life that continued during the performance. Whatever the case, everything was calculated to squeeze this kind of emotion out of the audience, and I certainly was an idiot for taking this staging seriously. The anxiety I was experiencing was nothing but mine; this is what we're taught all day long, and, deep down, I was trying to deny my feelings.

.Nothing worked. I remained convinced that the dancer's distress wasn't premeditated. The threat hovering over her wasn't sham. It wasn't I who was inventing the disastrous vibes emanating from her: I don't have such power. I took the arm of the woman I was going out with at the time, with whom I'd gone to the theater. But she didn't understand anything I was saying to her. She wanted to go to the ladies' room. I let her disappear into the crowd.

The dancer was about fifty feet from me. When I climbed onto the stage, it was stronger than me. Forget about the Théâtre de la Ville, Pina Bausch, respect for culture. In a second I was beside her. She was crying. Her eyes were closed, and she was crying. Her face was flooded with tears. Her nose was running, all the way to her lips and chin. Her features were terribly ferocious looking. I wasn't surprised. Even if I wasn't expecting anything precise, it was impossible that I'd been mistaken.

She hadn't heard me arrive, and I remained tongue-tied in front of her. In my mind, just my doing what I'd done should have been enough. Finally, I took her hand. I thought she was going to scream; but instead, she began squeezing my fingers with all her might. Her eyes remained closed, and she didn't open them at any moment. We didn't say a thing to each other. We stayed like that, face to face, holding hands, until the end of intermission.

She wasn't letting go. Her hand was crushing the bones in my fingers, and I responded by squeezing her hand as well. It was a kind of dialogue between us, for a tiresomely long time. It was enough for me to know that there was someone there for her, and it didn't matter that it was me. She had stopped crying, and her face was gradually becoming bearable. Behind me I heard the usherettes, commanding me in a low voice to leave the stage. They didn't dare come and get me.

It was only when the bell announced the end of intermission that the dancer let go of my hand. Without a word or a look, she disappeared stage left, as if she were flying above the floor. The dancer had reclaimed her rights. I went back to my seat. I pretended not to notice the people darting unpleasant looks in my direction. I was back with my date. "You always have to get noticed," she hissed between her teeth, while the lights fell and the performance, which I don't at all remember, began again.

How would I have been able to explain to her that this wasn't the first time I'd seen that dancer? At the time, I myself wasn't aware of it. And yet, ten years before, it really was she who, at the time, was twenty years older and was wandering through the night with a fantastic aura of bitterness.

I met her behind rue de Tilsitt. I wasn't yet sixteen and, without my parents knowing it, had gone out in the middle of the night, escaping by way of the balcony, after waiting with a beating heart for everybody at home to fall asleep. For two or three months I'd been giving everybody the slip that way. I was determined to meet life head on. It had taken me weeks to get the nerve to act on it. The first time, I'd only stayed outside for a few minutes, my stomach knotted at the thought that my absence might be discovered; and, in any case, I didn't know where to go at night. It was cold, and the rue Marbeuf was as silent and as disappointing as a desert. I'd gone back to bed.

But the unknown was summoning me. I was dreaming of encounters to end all encounters, of incredible sights. Shortly after, I began doing it again, this time getting as far as the Champs-Elysées. Immediately I felt inspired. It was full of lights and people who looked like they were living exciting experiences. The night seemed cheerful. Finally, I was out there. I was eager for everything, but I was walking quickly to give the impression that I knew where I was going so that I wouldn't attract attention. Then I went home and back to bed. No one had noticed my absence. But had I been caught, I wouldn't have regretted a thing because the emotions that I'd just experienced belonged to me.

Accordingly, I got into the habit of going out secretly as soon as I could. Though nothing much happened to me. Following chance noises, I didn't meet any people who gave me the desire to know them, when I didn't feel like getting away from them. I also learned that I'd need money to meet the city head on. I didn't give a damn. I went chasing the shadows and lights that were available, exhilarated by my nerve, alone in the end, and this freedom was euphoric enough. Getting away was already a complete adventure. Suddenly, time had stopped being repetitive. Everything was invested with a harsh, uncertain beauty, which those who were sleeping didn't even suspect. No matter how well I knew most of the streets that I took during the day, they became unrecognizable at night, quivering with unpredictability, and it was this metamorphosis that dazzled me. I felt alive. It was a big world.

Little by little, I also pushed back the limits, boldly going beyond Le Drugstore on the Champs-Elysées to explore the area around place de l'Étoile, and especially rue de Tilsitt, where I discovered half-nude crea-

tures calling out into the night. I knew they were prosti-
tutes, but that didn't mean anything to me. When I'd see
one climb into a car, my imagination would stop with
the slam of the door. She probably had to go to a party
where at the end everybody took a shower.

Some of them were so beautiful that they reminded
me of Madame Fenwick. I walked ceaselessly back and
forth in front of them, concealing my considerable lust
behind nonchalance that I faked so well, it even kept
me from ogling what I so desperately wanted to see close
up. Then it was too late, and I didn't turn back but kept
going as if I were strolling at the water's edge, but I was
feeling totally crestfallen and furious with myself.

Whenever one of these goddesses smiled at me, I
was ready to faint right then and there, as the thought
of what that could mean made all the blood rush out of
me. I planned next to hide my paltry sixteen years in
a deserted street, before retracing my steps like a wolf.
For a whole hour I could see from a distance one who
interested me. On the way back home, I carried her image with me like a promise that I then frantically kept
for myself, under my covers.

The next time, I would try to find her again; but she
had usually disappeared, and then another would attract

me. Because there was always one of them who would do, as far as I was concerned, and that obvious fact was thrilling. This was the way I fabricated wonderful nighttime encounters for myself, which kept my senses pricked for the rest of the week. Thanks to them, my life was excised of the pedestrian.

Once I saw something outrageous: a big blond, totally beside herself, was hurling insults at a man who was leaving without further ado. She had thrown her bag on the ground and was literally hopping up and down with rage, yelling and gesturing violently; you could tell that nothing could calm her down, and as she exploded completely and dangerously, was really losing it, she suddenly lifted her miniskirt and began to take off her panties, sliding them down her bare legs before throwing them far away and turning on her heels, her vagina in glorious display. Suddenly she calmed down. Pulling off her panties had lessened her anger, as if until that moment it had been located inside them. That night I went home thrilled but very baffled about what women have down there.

It was in the excitability of the night that I saw her: looking tiny on the street, she was staggering slightly under a light rain that had begun to fall unexpectedly, emptying the streets. She kept rummaging in her bag, which hindered her walk even more. Above all, there was that green hood, which she was snuggling into. A bottle-green one, which seemed to stand out from the night, as if to turn her into a ghost. More than toward her, it was toward it that I was walking. It seemed to want to say something, call to I don't know whom, shake up I don't know what. At the end of the street, a light turned green: it was like a sign; when it turned red again, I was almost expecting her to do so as well. Without knowing it, I was already ready to go through anything.

When I reached her, I continued past while I put on my famous unruffled look. But this time it was just too idiotic. I was through with passing things and people by. Letting everything get away from me. The street was deserted; I retraced my steps, and with a beating heart asked her if she'd lost something. I would have liked to find something less stupid to say, in a deeper voice, but coming up to her was already an immense achievement. She barely looked at me and grumbled some words that I didn't understand. I came closer. She must have been about fifty. Maybe less. The rain was plastering her hair to her head, and there was something sad about her shoulders.

When she turned to face me, I was struck by the intensity of her face. Her mouth smiled, but her eyes looked as if they were crying, it was an insane expression, as if her features were disputing a disaster, you would have said that everything in her had been turned inside out like a glove to expose its hypersensitivity, cry for help or something, laugh in your face, or overflow with humanity. Never had I seen a face so irreparable. At the same time, her hood gaped open at her chest and I immediately saw that she was practically naked underneath, her breast stuck out, heaven-sent, a breast that was completely flat and lifeless, like a crushed pancake, but I couldn't have cared less.

This breast being offered was madness. I couldn't help eyeing it, and as if recovering from a long stiffness of a joint, my entire body got pins and needles all over, just by glancing at it. That's when I stopped being my age. I had gotten hard, it wouldn't stop poking against my trousers, and a disturbing twitching was pumping it up. Never had I felt such an emulsion of my being. Those sessions under the covers were nothing compared to this.

I was afraid that she'd notice something. She mustn't know. I don't know what she would have thought. Would have been afraid, or worse. Would have immediately straightened her clothes. So I remained in front of her without doing anything, engaging in conversation as if it was nothing. As if everything was normal: she, me, her maddening nudity in the night, and the limitless feeling that electrified me every time I laid eyes on her breast spilling from her chest.

She barely heard me, was more concerned with the contents of her bag than my words. Good. I could look at her shamelessly. I was only asking that she not look at me. I didn't want her to see me. I didn't want anyone looking except me.

At one point, I told her that she looked like Little Green Riding Hood. She responded with a brief little-girl laugh. "Then you're the wolf," she joked. She wasn't taking me seriously, and I felt ridiculous. Her voice was weak, thickened. A dab of saliva was stuck to the corner of her lips and I was fascinated by it. It was as if something small and disgusting was giving me a sign. The blood in my veins was galvanizing.

I had not the slightest idea of what I wanted. I didn't want anything. I only wanted to stay with her. To keep her from leaving was all that I wanted. I didn't want her to go, no, she wasn't going to disappear like the others, not her, not this time. It was still raining, and I said it would be better to find shelter in the entranceway of a building, she'd get drenched. But she wasn't listening. She didn't seem to be well. She swayed from side to side and sometimes closed her eyes, then suddenly opened them wide and looked around incredulously.

At one point I told myself to leave her alone. But instead of that, I brought my hand to her face and touched her cheek. I was trembling. She didn't react. I got bolder. I threaded my fingers through her wet hair and pulled it gently at the root. My movements seemed to know what they were doing all by themselves. I made her head move slightly from side to side. She closed her eyes. She was at my mercy.

So I kissed her neck, her cheek, everywhere on her face, half-licking her, drinking in her features. I no longer knew what I was doing. I found her lips. She opened them. It was warm, incredible. At the same time, my hands grabbed her breasts, squeezed them, devoured them. I couldn't stop. My penis was going wild in my trousers. I pinned her against the car. She let me do it. I was choked with emotion and drew back to get my breath. I studied her: she was naked from the waist up, her hood fell onto her shoulders, she was looking at me strangely, everything was of an indescribable beauty.

Still caressing her breasts, I began to say anything at all to her. Seeing my hands moving over her skin drove me crazy. I would have wanted them to sink into her flesh, ripping apart her jutting ribs, move beyond her body, exceed everything. She broke away a bit and said in a glum voice that she had to leave. I didn't listen to her. I didn't want to hear it. She mustn't say a word. Only my hands existed. My hands that were undressing her, looking for I didn't know what that would shatter the earth. Make me immortal.

I kissed her eagerly. She didn't step back. Everything about her was limp. I pushed her against the car again. I no longer had control over anything. I grabbed her hand and put it on my penis. I wanted to show her. So she'd know. So she'd take my cock and squeeze it with all her strength and I didn't know what else. At the same time I tried to spread her thighs apart. I wanted to know. Everything in me was getting carried away. I bit her neck. She let out a tiny cry. She belonged to me. When I heard her murmur, "Not you. No. Not you."

It was as if I'd been slapped. I let go of her immediately. She'd spoken with a voice that was terribly weary. What did she mean, not me? Why not me? I didn't know where I was anymore. Everything in the street was wavering. I saw her picking up her bag, which had fallen to the ground. What, me? Did she know something that I didn't? What was there about me in particular? That made her say it.

But she had already moved away and was crossing the street while making an effort to walk straight. I didn't understand. She hadn't understood anything. It wasn't what she thought. I loved her. I wanted to live with her. I saw her hail a taxi. It wasn't possible. Running, I caught up with her. I reached her as she was sitting in the back seat. I wanted to see her again. Please. I took her hand. She told me that it was no big deal. Another time. Her hand squeezed my arm. I became aware of the driver of the taxi and let go. She closed the door. I remained on the sidewalk. I no longer knew who I was. Me? Who was that?

For entire nights I looked for her everywhere. I went all over the neighborhood, endlessly. I was sure she'd come back. She must be looking for me as well. She couldn't have forgotten me.

Once I got the nerve to ask in a bar that was open all night if anybody had seen a woman dressed in a green hood. I had to explain what I meant by the word. An odious smile passed into the eyes of the bartender. I never found her again.

In high school, I spent a long time drawing in margins the face of a woman whose mouth was smiling and whose eyes were crying. I still have some of the sketches. My grades became disastrous. I didn't believe in anything anymore. Neither day nor night had fulfilled me. Madame Fenwick had disappeared, and the woman in the hood hadn't wanted me. The sun and the moon had both slipped away at the last moment, in the same way. What was there to reach out to? I had no place anywhere. What was wrong with me?

Sometimes, before going to sleep, I'd picture Madame Fenwick and the woman in the hood; they entwined and began to caress each other; but suddenly they began to devour each other, and everything finally turned to carnage. They couldn't both stay in the same scene, just as day and night are irreducible. At what moment had the error slipped in? I wanted answers.

While doing English homework, I came up with the idea that the death penalty was preferable to life in prison. The English teacher graded my paper with rage. In front of the whole class, she decided to make it an example not to follow. She wasn't only trying to teach us English, and that as well made me think about literature. I answered her by saying that my point of view wasn't that of the judge, but of the condemned. "You cannot understand," I told her insolently, in English. She kicked me out of class and threw all my belongings in the hallway.

I stopped going out on the sly. From then on, I spent all my nights with my ear pressed to a little portable radio I'd stolen from a store. One time I tuned in on a debate. "You can't play the angel to deny death the way you can play the idiot to forget about it; nonetheless, the fact remains that we're human beings, and if we begin with that, there's something to find," said a voice. I memorized that sentence by heart.

On another night, a man recounted that he'd totally failed at his professional life but perfectly succeeded at his sex life. Under my covers, I was baffled. Then there could be several lives, and not just one, and these separate lives were competing with each other? Even devouring each other? Why?

It took two more years for me to end up in bed with a girl. It doesn't at all happen as expected: no matter how much I poke at her, I can't penetrate her, my penis butts desperately against a bone without ever finding the entrance. It's diabolical. I tell myself that we must not love each other enough. There's no other explanation. My love isn't worthy of doing it. I'm mortified. But there's nothing that can be done, she's every bit as inexperienced as I am, and I end up forgetting about it, hiding my sputtering penis and repressing an acidic, piercing pain in my lower abdomen.

It will take me some time to understand that you have to use your hands to help in the penetration. I didn't know it was allowed. I'd never seen this done anywhere, neither in a film nor in a book: all the stories to which I had access humiliated reality. So love wasn't enough, you also needed technique. That was the road that pleasure took. I wasn't an angel.

On that day, I understood that life began where images ended. At the place where I'd had to improvise and had been left to myself, without any description coming before my acts to tell them how to proceed. In a bedroom, the adventure became mine for once: it was about invention, starting with the self, whatever your state of mind might be. Finally being present, in body and in mind, wholly daring. I've never perceived sexual adventure as either a social practice or a formality required by nature, but as one of the rare possibilities that I had to devote myself with someone to a human experience that goes beyond me (in times of peace).

Recently, a very young girl, on the first evening, took from her bag a little vial for lubricating her anus. Not that she was particularly into it, but she figured that all men liked it, and "you have to do everything when it comes to sex," she said. Her "have to" was excessive. At not even twenty, she knew a thousand times more than me at her age, and, in comparison, my youth seemed very naive. However, it seems to me that it was still a matter of the same ignorance about sex, which had merely become terribly performance oriented. When she fell asleep, she sucked her thumb.

AGE SEVENTEEN. With my parents, I go out to dinner one evening at Pub Renault, on the Champs-Elysées, as we usually do when we're in the money. In the courtyard of the building, while my father is taking his time on the stairway, I suddenly embrace my mother and kiss her on the mouth; far from refusing, her tongue finds mine. It's a long, salacious kiss between us. My hand caresses her back, then her buttocks. A part of me is watching me do it and not participating in the action. Recording the slightest detail. We separate before my father turns up.

When he appears, my mother merrily slips her arm under his. She kisses him on the check and quickly leads him along while casting furtive glances toward the concierge's office and the windows of the building. In front of me, she wiggles her hips a little.

In the street, I'm waiting to be struck dead by lightning, at any moment. I watch the sky to see whether it's coming down on my head; I *actually* watch the sky. But no, nothing is happening, not the slightest flash, no sign, no intervention. Not even a pigeon crushed before my eyes. The clouds are the same as always. The cars stop at the red light. They start up again at the green. Father and Mother use the crosswalk. I follow them. My action hasn't changed a thing. Everything has remained in place. The world is the same, and I'm its prisoner. My intervention didn't accomplish anything. Didn't cause any upheaval. It's always the same oppressive emptiness. The same time, in repetition. The same death in life. It's still me.

Two or three days later, my mother tells me gravely, "You have to forget what happened the other day. It was a moment of madness. You understand." I understand. "But why did you do that in the courtyard?" She'd like to know. From the tone of her voice, I can tell it's the only question that concerns her. As if it were a flaw in what just happened. Kissing her in the courtyard shocks her rather than the fact that I kissed her at all.

Twenty years later, I go to see my father in the country and tell him about that scene. We're walking on a dirt path, as in the photo with the scalloped edges. He says, "These things happen."

I figure I've seen it all when, getting home one evening, among various messages, I recognize my father's voice on my answering machine. It sounds awkward, as it always does when he's speaking into empty space. He says, "Hello . . . Grégoire . . . It's Dad . . . Sorry to bother you, but your mother just jumped out the window . . . I'm here with the medics. We're leaving for the hospital right way . . . Okay. I wanted to let you know. I'm calling you with the news. Much love. Later."

I'm standing next to the answering machine. I've stopped breathing. I close my eyes. Inside I'm repeating, "Not that. No. Not that." It's like a scream that I can't get out. I can feel the silence in the room. Coming from the courtyard of the building through the open window. It's mild weather outside. He hasn't said what her condition is. If she was dead or not. Suddenly I see an image of her crushed body. Five floors. I reopen my eyes. I look at the wall in front of me. Place my two hands flat on the stone. I don't know what to do. No gesture seems enough. He didn't even say which hospital. Let's hope she's dead. Anything, rather than living and in a thousand pieces. Reduced to a torso. Maybe less than a torso. I close my eyes. So she finally did it. I bang my head against the wall several times.

Then I wait in darkness for my father to call. I have all that time to picture my mother after a five-story fall. One hundred fifty feet, that's what it must be. In a straight line, that's about what it is.

She's at Hôpital Saint-Antoine. She's alive. Nothing wrong. Not even a broken arm. A cracked rib. Only a compression of the vertebrae. In two or three days she should be able to get out, once all the exams are over. For the moment she's sleeping. The doctors can't get over it. They've never seen such a thing happen. They talk about a miracle. "From that height, usually nothing's left," the intern on duty tells me.

She crashed into the zinc roof of a small shed, which absorbed the impact of her fall. Leaning out the window, you can make out the imprint left there of her body in fetal position, like a mold into which you could pour plaster. As I close the window, it occurs to me that defying laws seems to be a specialty in my family.

My father and I keep watch over her for part of the night. My mother is lying on a bed behind a blue curtain. There's nothing we can do, so we leave to get a bite in the first brasserie that we see. My father explains that this time he arrived too late to grab her. He can't get over what she did. He almost seems to admire it.

The next day, we go back to see her. My mother's eyes open a crack. Her face is deathly pale and at the same time very smooth. She takes my hand. She murmurs, "Even death doesn't want me." I come up with a vague smile. Just as well, I tell her.

GRÉGOIRE BOUILLIER is the editor of
a scientific magazine and author
of *The Mystery Guest*. Originally a
painter, he published his first book
at age forty. He has one daughter
and lives in Paris, France.